An invitation to our reader:
Most of the routes in the GUIDE
have been contributed by veteran
cyclists who ride the area regularly.
But, due to construction and the
flood of '93, the roads are constant-
ly changing. With all our careful
editing, we acknowledge that there
may still be some mistakes. If you
find an error or know of any
improvement, please let us know.
We welcome your comments and
suggestions.

Address all correspondence to:
Guide To Cycling St. Louis
c/o Cycle Write Enterprises
P.O. Box 26243
Shawnee Mission, KS 66225

Library of Congress
Cataloging-in-Publication Data
CIP 94-094227
Katz, Steve
96 bicycle tours in and around
St. Louis
ISBN 0-9632730-2-7

Published by
Cycle Write Enterprises
Shawnee Mission, Kansas 66225
Printed in the United States of
America

Text by Steve Katz
Maps by Mike Ogden
Book design by Randy Seba
Cover photograph by Phil
Shoulberg
Cartoons & caricatures by Bob Bliss

GUIDE TO CYCLINGSTLOUIS

By
STEVE KATZ

4

TABLE OF CONTENTS

FOREWORD

Compiling GUIDE TO CYCLING ST. LOUIS involved two unique challenges

First, as both the author and publisher, I was not a native St. Louisan and, therefore, I had little familiarity with the area. I called upon local cyclists, who, not only willingly shared their favorite routes with me, but also, introduced me to other friends in this wonderful St. Louis cycling community. Most of these contributors are profiled throughout the guide and many are pictured on the cover. The publication of Guide To Cycling St. Louis was the combined effort of many dedicated cyclists.

The second challenge was the flood of '93 which made virtually all maps and many cycling routes obsolete. During the publication of the guide in the winter of 1993-94, many of the areas were being reconstructed, including the KATY Trail. We've attempted to designate where routes are still under repair. We intend for this Guide to be effective for several seasons and, therefore, we ask your patience and your understanding.

While the popularity of bicycling is very much on the upswing in both St. Louis and the nation, the availability of "safe" country roads is being reduced by urban sprawl. Take the long popular St. Albans area as an example. It's become more and more difficult to use our bicycles as transportation because of increased distances between home and the workplace plus heavier rush hour traffic adds to the burden. This Guide has attempted to be sensitive to this problem by noting the times when a route is less congested.

Since we are obliged to share the road with motorists, we ask two favors of our readers. Please always wear a helmet and encourage kids to do the same. And, when a motorist is rude and there's that temptation to express your anger negatively, just smile and wave back.

This book is printed on Recycled Paper.

Guide To Cycling St. Louis is published solely for the enhancement of your cycling pleasure. While all routes have been cycled many times, the Guide does not imply that they are safe. Safety is the responsibility of every cyclist. There are certain times of the day and certain days of the week that are safer times to cycle a particular route. Please factor this into your plans.

There are a variety of things that attract us to cycling, including exercise, companionship, adventure, challenge, independence, and so on. In the decade that I've cycled I've realized many more benefits than I ever dreamed existed. Today, I use my experiences plus the friends I've made cycling, to act in the role as an advocate, as a positive voice for cycling. There are three developments I'd like to see happen in the future to improve our cycling way of life.

1. Stripe and sign existing "bicycle friendly" roads and bridges by using the Share-the-Road logo.
2. Consider all new road and bridge construction for bicycle use in the initial planning stages.
3. Incorporate bicycle programs into schools, starting early, to establish the right attitudes and behavior. (See BicycleWorks story next page)

These are my hopes for the future. I always welcome those of others. Share your hopes and dreams with me, and together we can work to make St. Louis an even better place to ride a bicycle.

Happy Cycling,

Steve Katz

Steve Katz
Author/Publisher
CYCLE WRITE ENTERPRISES

ACKNOWLEDGMENTS

It will be sincerely stated several times throughout this guide that this is a project by cyclists for cyclists. A special thanks to each and every one of you. Some of you were cheerleaders, offering words of encouragement. Others provided the maps and routes without which this guide would not have been possible. With so many people to whom we're indebted, it's possible we have inadvertently left out some names. Please forgive the oversight and consider yourself an important part of this book.

Linda Addy - OAC/AYH
Bob Alsobrook - OAC/AYH
Larry Brinker - Break Away Bicycle Tours
Claus Dieter Claussen - St. Louis Cycling Club
Kathy Garrity
Bob Gunther - BABES
Jim Jeske - OAC/AYH
Kathy Kaiser
Jim Klages
Ray Latimer - BABES
Paul Moskovitz
Ted Meyer
Becky Powell - OAC/AYH

Dave Reiter
Marilyn Roberts - St. Louis Cycling Club
Paul Shoulberg - Cover Photo
Carol Tosie
Beth Trautman - American Diabetes Assn.
Gene Trost
Barb Troy - Rivercity Pedallers
Brian Vanderheyden
Jack Welch - OAC/AYH
John Werner - BABES
Dave Weidler - BABES
Sue Wilhlem - OAC/AYH
Jo Wilhemi
Dick Willis OAC/AYH
Wayne Witter - BABES

Julie Wynn - Missouri Meanders
Tom Yarbrough - Touring Society
K.C. GROUP
Chris Bassett - Displays
Paul Raymond - Graphic Services
Bob Bliss - Cartoons & Caricatures
Scott Cotter - Editing
Lynda Logan - Support Services
Mike Ogden - Maps
Randy Seba - Graphics and Computer services
Doug Schofield - Displays

The story of St. Louisan Roy Bohn and his BicycleWorks is an excellent example of what can happen with a program that establishes good attitudes and healthy behavior in youngsters. Beginning in a garage in 1988, BicycleWorks has been offering 9-17 year old underprivileged youth incentives for education and improved performance. Instead of providing "a handout" for these kids, BicycleWorks has an after school program that offers jobs in bicycle repair with the proper training. Performance is not measured on a competitive basis, but on an individual basis. The reward is a chance for a youngster to earn a recycled (used) bicycle.
BicycleWorks is a non-profit community education organization which welcomes donations of your time and talents, bicycles and financial support. (314) 664-0828

HISTORY OF ST. LOUIS CYCLING

The history of St. Louis cycling begins with the formation of The St. Louis Cycling Club in June of 1887 at the Lindell Hotel in downtown St. Louis. The Club was organized around "the pursuit of friendship and togetherness ... and had well-attended club runs into the surrounding counties each weekend." In the early days the Club was primarily a touring club, although it included a few who also raced.

The history of St. Louis cycling closely parallels that of American cycling. The League of American Wheelmen (LAW), the nation's first and oldest bicycle advocacy group, fought for cyclists' rights and was recognized for its Good Roads Campaign. In the 1890s, cycling experienced what many consider a "golden age". At that time the League boasted a membership of nearly 100,000 cyclists.

But, the success of the League's Good Roads Campaign, together with the advent of automobiles and trolleys, brought about a decline in cycling.

Manufacturers and consumers came to consider the bicycle as a toy rather than a means of transportation, an attitude the would prevail until the Great Depression. Except for an occasional paper boy or a telegraph messenger boy, bicycles became the province of the kids.

During the early 1900s, the St. Louis Cycling Club's hard-core members abandoned their expensive clubhouse to take up "headquarters in the saddle", which became the club's slogan. Today, the focus of the St. Louis Cycling club is primarily that of racing.

Cycling, as a means of transportation in both St. Louis and the U.S., experienced only brief upturns during World War II and during the energy crisis of the 1970s. In 1974, Dick Leary of the Ozark Area Council/ AYH, organized the Moonlight Ramble.

This classic ride after dark through downtown St. Louis would grow to become the largest bicycle event of its kind in the nation.

Technology was a significant factor in again developing an interest in bicycling. In 1972, Raleigh and Schwinn introduced extension brake levers. This innovation attracted adults to cycling after an absence of many decades. At this same time, the St. Louis Cycling Club, and the Ozark Area Council AYH, were joined by the Touring Cyclist which launched the St. Louis Bicycle Touring Society in 1979.

A history of St. Louis cycling would be remiss without the mention of Natalie Kekeisen. As an AYH member, Natalie led Tuesday rides and cycled about 10,000 miles a year.

She organized an alternative to AYH's annual CAMP ride (Cycle Across Missouri Parks) called the CATSUP ride (Cycle Across The State University & Parks). The annual Flat As A Pancake Ride is a tribute to Natalie Kekeisen.

This brief history, contributed by area cyclists, only scratches the surface of significant events and people who have shaped the cycling community of St. Louis.

It would be impossible to list the achievements made by all the individuals who had a hand in making cycling in St. Louis what it is today. One thing is certain, the history of bicycling in St. Louis is a long and proud one.

Shakespeare said, "What's past is prologue". It's difficult to know in which direction we're headed without knowing first where we've been." The rich tradition of St. Louis cycling should insure that the future is a bright one.

The challenges of urbanization and the flood of 1993 have both become opportunities rather than obstacles for such advocacy groups as the Missouri Bicycle Federation, Gateway Trailnet, the St. Louis Bicycle Touring Society, Ozark Area Council AYH, and others. New trails including The KATY Trail and designated mountain bike areas create recreation and transportation venues for all members of the family to enjoy.

This is an open invitation to every cyclist to give something back to cycling in your community.

HOW TO USE THIS GUIDE

Guide to Cycling St. Louis has been copyrighted. *Each map and graphic as it appears in this Guide is the property of Cycle Write Enterprises.* Because of its size and format, we're aware that carrying the Guide on your bicycle is a *weighty* problem. Therefore, we encourage you to copy individual maps for your own personal use and enjoyment. Mark or highlight the maps for difficult passages. We just want to avoid seeing reproductions of the Guide or even sections of it for commercial use.

The guide is divided into five sections:

➪ St. Charles County

➪ West County

➪ Metro-Central including North & South County

➪ Metro-East

➪ Other

The starting point of a ride determines into which sector a ride is placed. For example, if an entire ride is in St. Charles County, but starts in Chesterfield, it will be listed among West County rides.

Since almost all rides are on public roads, the Guide defers the responsibility for safety to you. Obviously, conditions vary with the weather, the traffic, the days of week, and the time of the day. All these factors have been carefully con-sidered in selecting rides for this Guide.

If you're an inexperienced cyclist or new to St. Louis, we urge you to join one of the cycling organizations listed on page 123 or to try an orga-nized ride. In addition to the Bike Clubs and tour groups, we have included a listing of Bicycle Dealers to aid in pur-chasing a new bicycle or in servicing the one you already own. These bicycle shops are both capable and willing to suggest routes to try and organizations to join.

Most cyclists tend to "ride in their own backyard". We sug-gest you use this Guide to explore other areas. The St. Louis Bicycle Touring Society has regularly scheduled rides during season at 6:00 PM as follows: Monday-St. Charles; Tuesday-Jefferson Barracks; Wednesday-Clayton; Thursday-Fairview Heights. AYH also has regularly scheduled rides in all areas of St. Louis. This is an excellent way to learn new routes and meet new people. The other groups listed under organized rides have weekday, evening, and weekend rides to meet your needs. It's no exaggera-tion to say that during the cycling season, there's at least one ride each day in the St. Louis area.

We hope that Guide To Cycling St. Louis will become your passport to new, exciting, and adventuresome bicycling in the St. Louis area.

O.K.... SO YOU WON'T WEAR A HELMET... BUT WILL YOU SIGN THIS ORGAN DONOR CARD?

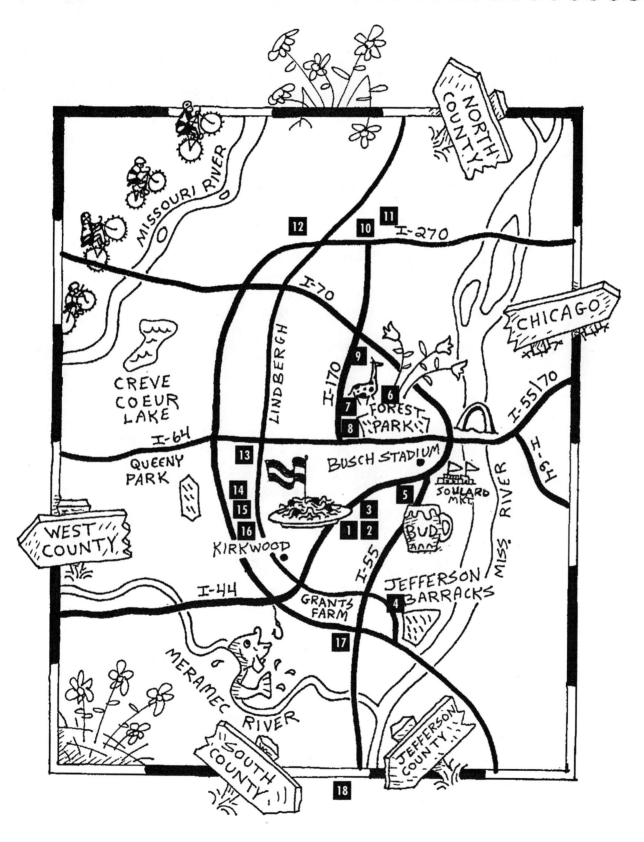

PAUL
MOSKOVITZ

began his cycling in 1969 as an Indianapolis teenager. Club rides led to racing, then touring and ultra marathon events. In 1985 with a friend, Paul co-founded and coached the St. Louis Rockits Racing Team. He maintains a collection of rides, newsletters, and memorabilia of St. Louis cycling. Paul would like to some day see a new velodrome as a part of the St. Louis County Park Department.

JIM
JESKE

got started in cycling in 1984 as a volunteer for AYH's Bike Across Missouri. Jim rode BAM the next two years. On two different occasions he was crew member for cyclists participating in Race Across America. Jim's talents were recognized when he was elected President of the National Bicycle Tour Directors Association for 1992-1993. He enjoys cycling for the people, the exercise, and the great outdoors. Jim shares our hopes that the entire Missouri cycling community will join forces to promote a happier, healthier atmosphere.

WHAT THE HECK IS A BEE TREE?

Starting Point: Wilmore Park, intersection of Gravois & Hampton
Distance: 35 Miles
Approximate Pedaling Time: 3 Hours
Terrain: Rolling
Things To See: This ride was contributed by Bob Alsobrook. Ride through Jefferson Barracks. Bee Tree Park has scenic overlook of the Mississippi River.

Cycle from Wilmore Park
RIGHT on Hampton
RIGHT on Broadway into Jefferson Barracks Park on Gregg
RIGHT at Sherman
LEFT at Boundry
RIGHT on Sappington Barracks
LEFT on Telegram
RIGHT at Kinswood
LEFT at Ringer which turns into Yeager

RIGHT on Milburn
LEFT on Old Baumgartner Rd
RIGHT at Telegraph
LEFT at Christopher Rd
RIGHT on Becker
LEFT on Finestown Rd into Bee Tree Park
RETURN:
RIGHT on Becker out of park
RIGHT on Telepgraph
RIGHT at Sappington Barracks Rd
LEFT at Boundry
RIGHT on Sherman
LEFT on Gregg thru Jefferson Barracks to Broadway
LEFT at Marceau to Wilmore Park and starting point

FROM SOUTH ST. LOUIS TO JEFFERSON BARRACKS

Starting Point: Hampton &
Gravois Avenues
Distance: 16 miles
Approximate Pedaling Time:
1-1.5 hours
Terrain: Mostly flat
Things To See: This is a
beginners ride

Cycle north
on Hampton Ave
LEFT on Jamieson
LEFT at Eichelberger
RIGHT at McCausland Ave
LEFT on Wabash Ave
LEFT on Lansdowne Ave
LEFT on Willmore Park bike
path parallel to River des Peres
Blvd
Continue on Carondelet Blvd
after crossing Morganford Rd
LEFT at Alabama Ave
RIGHT at Davis St
RIGHT on Broadway into
Jefferson Barracks Park
Cycle clockwise and exit park
on Broadway
LEFT on Marceau St
RIGHT at Alabama Ave
LEFT at Germania St across I-
55 which becomes Hampton
Ave after crossing
Gravois Ave
Return to starting point

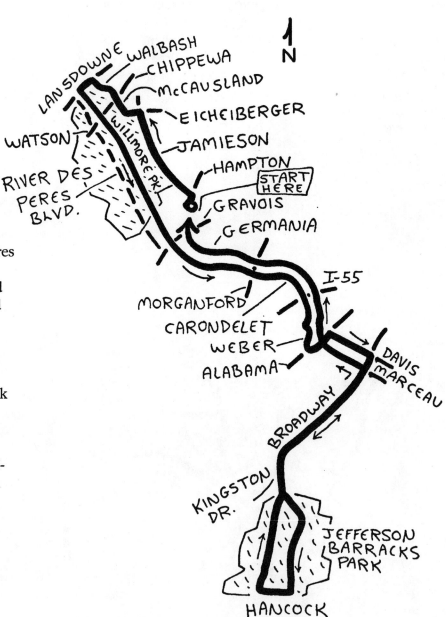

WILLMORE PARK TO JEFFERSON BARRACKS

Starting Point: Willmore Park, Germania & Hampton Ave
Distance: 22 miles
Approximate Pedaling Time: 2 hours
Terrain: Mostly flat
Things To See: Willmore Park, Tower Grove Park, Carondelet Park, and Jefferson Barracks.

Cycle from Willmore Park, right on Germania crossing I-55
RIGHT on Broadway to Jefferson Barracks Park
LEFT on Grant
LEFT at Hancock Ave
RIGHT at Gregg for clockwise loop.
Exit Park on Broadway across Marceau St
LEFT on Longborough Ave
RIGHT at Carondelet Park on Grand Blvd
RIGHT at Holly Hills Ave
LEFT on Michigan Ave
RIGHT on Louisiana Blvd
RIGHT at Grand St
LEFT at Virginia Ave
LEFT on Meramec
RIGHT on Spring Ave
LEFT at Tower Grove Park on Arsenal across Kingshighway
RIGHT and then LEFT at Reber Place
LEFT on Sublette crossing Chippewa and becoming Macklind Ave
RIGHT on Longborough Ave
LEFT at Jamieson Ave to Willmore Park

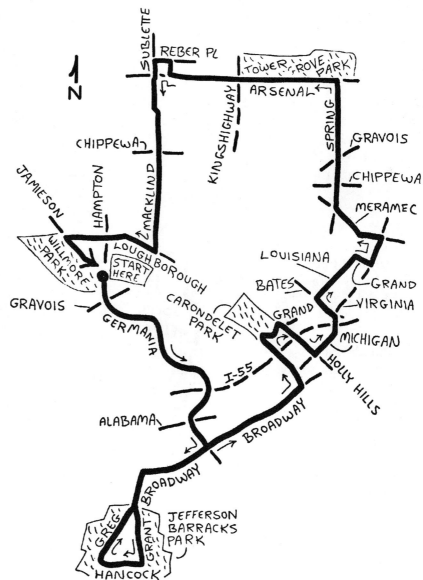

A TOUR OF "THE HILL"

Starting Point: Jefferson Barracks, Connie's concession stand
Distance: 32 Miles
Approximate Pedaling Time: 2.5-3 Hours
Terrain: Flat, except for The Hill
Things To See: The Hill, so called because it's the highest point in St. Louis county, is the location of many fine Italian restaurants, including Amighetti's for lunch; save room for Ted Drewe's frozen custard on the return trip.

Bob Alsobrook shares the view of many of us that we cycle to support our eating and drinking habits. For that reason alone, the ride to "The Hill" is a must.

Cycle from Connie's at Jefferson Barracks Park south on Grant
RIGHT on Kearney
RIGHT on Gregg
LEFT at Broadway
LEFT at Bates
RIGHT on Compton
RIGHT on Walsh
LEFT at Minnesota
LEFT at Delor
RIGHT on Compton
LEFT on Utah across Gravois
RIGHT at Gustine
LEFT at Wyoming
RIGHT on Morganford
LEFT on Arsenal across Hampton and Watson
RIGHT at Clifton and regroup at Clifton Park
RIGHT on Southwest

LEFT on Tamm
RIGHT on Odell
LEFT at Ivanhoe across Arsenal
RIGHT at Fyler
LEFT on Jamieson
LEFT on Loughborough
LEFT at Macklind which runs into Sublette
RIGHT at Bischoff
LEFT on Marconi to Amighetti's
LEFT on Wilson
LEFT at Macklind
LEFT at Arsenal

RIGHT on Morgunford, watch out for grate
LEFT on Wyoming
RIGHT at Gustine
LEFT at Utah
RIGHT on Spring
LEFT on Meramec
RIGHT at Compton
LEFT at Delor
RIGHT on Nebraska
RIGHT onto Broadway and follow Grant into Jefferson Barracks Park

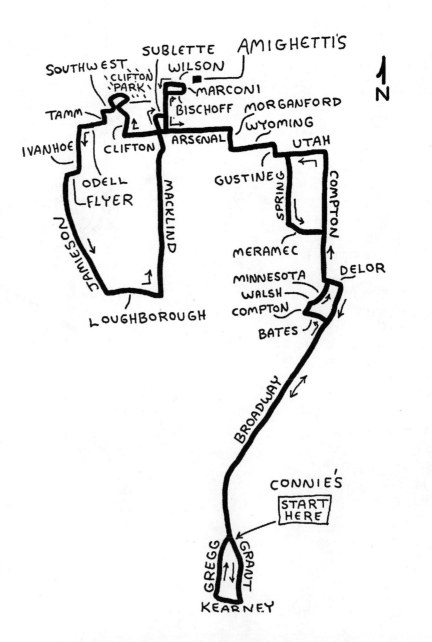

18

TOWER GROVE PARK TO HICKEY PARK

Starting Point: Tower Grove Park
Distance: 23 miles
Approximate Pedaling Time: 2-2.5 hours
Terrain: Flat
Things To See: Tower Grove Park, Anheuser Busch brewery, Soulard Market, Gateway Arch, and David Hickey Park

Cycle from Tower Grove Park
LEFT on Kingshighway
RIGHT on Magnolia
RIGHT at Arkansas Ave
LEFT at Pestalozzi St past Anheuser Busch
LEFT on Broadway crossing under I-55 and I-40
Continue on 4th St past the Arch
Continue north on Broadway crossing McKinley Bridge ramp and Grand Blvd to David Hickey Park
Return the same way.

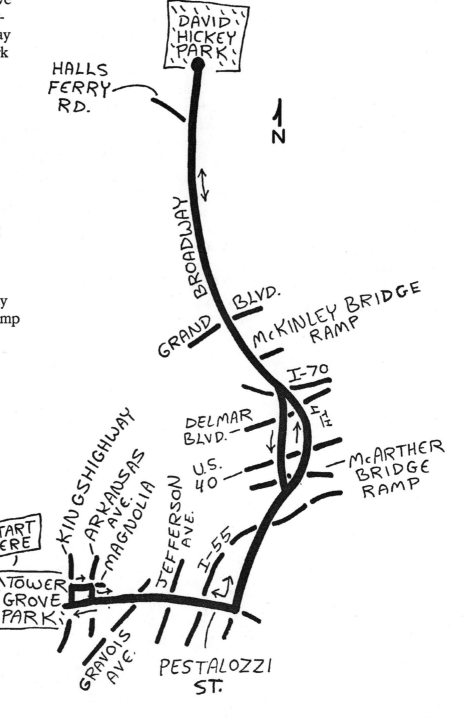

LEISURELY CITY RIDE

Starting Point: Jefferson Memorial at Forest Park
Distance:
Approximate Pedaling Time:
Terrain: Flat city ride; traffic depends upon time of day
Things To See: Soulard Market, Anheuser Busch Brewery, Botanical Gardens (free admission Wed. and Sat. mornings), The Hill for lunch, optional route to Crown Candy Kitchen and Union Station. This is a BABES ride from David Weidler.

Cycle from Jefferson Memorial counter clockwise on bike path.
LEFT on Oakland
RIGHT on Tamm
LEFT at Park
RIGHT at Pierce
LEFT on Manchester
RIGHT on Sublette

LEFT at Wilson (Amighetti's for lunch)
LEFT at Marconi
RIGHT on Shaw (O'Connel's Pub)
LEFT on Kingshighway
RIGHT at Shaw Blvd to Missouri Botanical Gardens
RIGHT at Tower Grove Ave
LEFT on bike path
LEFT on Pestalozzi
RIGHT at Compton
LEFT at Arsenal
LEFT on Jefferson
RIGHT on Pestalozzi to Anheuser Busch Brewery
LEFT at 9th past Russell to Soulard Market
RIGHT at Lafayette
RIGHT on 8th
RIGHT on Russell
RIGHT at Mississippi
LEFT at Park Ave
RIGHT on California
LEFT on Chouteau
RIGHT at Vandeventer
LEFT at Clayton Ave

RIGHT on Forest Park Bike Path to starting point

Option for dessert
RIGHT at Grand Ave
RIGHT at W. Pine
RIGHT on Boyle
LEFT on Laclede
RIGHT on Compton
LEFT at Market
LEFT at Tucker (12th)
LEFT on 13th
LEFT on N. Florissant
RIGHT at Union Station and Crown Candy Co
Return same route except
RIGHT on Olive from 12th
LEFT on Ewing
RIGHT at Laclede and follow same route to Forest Park

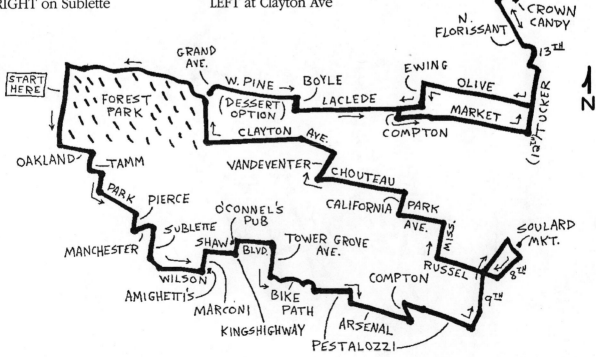

20

WASHINGTON UNIVERSITY TO THE SMOKEHOUSE

Starting Point: North end of Washington U. campus, corner of Forsyth & Skinker
Distance:
Approximate Pedaling Time:
Terrain: Gently rolling
Things To See: Paul Moskcovitz says this is a fun way for urban cyclists to see the country and get some good food at The Smoke House

Cycle west on Forsyth across Big Bend
RIGHT on Jackson across Delmar
LEFT at Amherst
RIGHT at Hanley
LEFT on Blackberry which dead-ends at golf course
LEFT on Groby (Old Bonhomme)

LEFT at Heather Hill
RIGHT at Stacy Drive, ride around barricade
LEFT on Warson Rd (south)
RIGHT on Clayton Rd crossing Lindbergh
RIGHT at Spoede
LEFT at Conway
RIGHT on Chesterfield Parkway (oasis) across Hwy 40
RIGHT on Chesterfield Airport Rd to The Smoke House
Return the same route

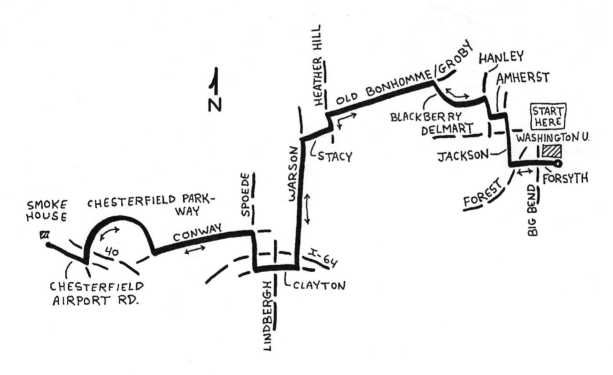

BASICALLY A BAGEL RIDE

Starting Point: The Touring Cyclist in Richmond Heights
Distance:18 miles
Approximate Pedaling Time:1.5-2 hours
Terrain: Mostly flat
Things To See: This is a Touring Society ride. It's a chance for a loop around Forest Park and a"refueling" at Basically Bagels

Cycle from Touring Cyclist on Big Bend
RIGHT at Clayton Rd
LEFT at Skinker and decide upon a loop of Forest Park now or on return trip
RIGHT on Grand Drive across Kingshighway becoming West Pine
RIGHT on Taylor to Basically Bagels on Euclid near West Pine.
The return route is the same.

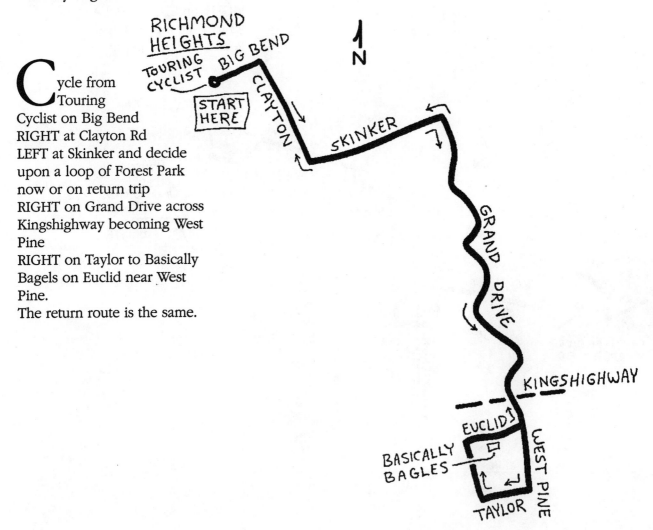

RIDE TO LONE ELK PARK

Starting Point: Heman Park in University City, Olive St & Midland
Distance: 40 Miles
Approximate Pedaling Time: 3-3.5 Hours
Terrain: Moderately hilly
Things To See: An urban ride says Bob Alsobrook. An out and back ride to Lone Elk Park where the Chubb Trail starts.

Cycle south on Midland from Heman Park
LEFT at Delmar
RIGHT at Big Bend for some distance
LEFT into Marshall Rd before I-270 overpass
LEFT on Hwy 141
RIGHT on N. Outer Rd into Lone Elk Park
Stay RIGHT and cycle counterclockwise around the park
Return the same route to the starting point in Heman Park.

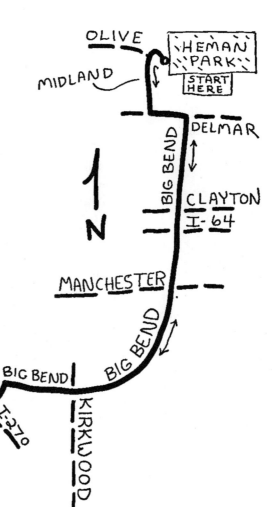

FLORISSANT TO ST. CHARLES LOOP

Starting Point: I-270 pedestrian crossover, intersection of Lafayette St and Dunn Rd
Distance: 20 miles
Approximate Pedaling Time: 1.5 Hours
Terrain: Moderately flat except hill at bluff
Things To See: An interesting ride descending and ascending the bluffs from Ted Meyer. A view of the Missouri River bottoms and Old St. Charles.

Starting from the pedestrian crossover of I-270 at Lafayette Street and Dunn Road
Cycle west on Pershall Rd crossing Lindberg Blvd and continue on Utz Lane
LEFT at Fee Fee Rd watching for a quick right and then left turn
RIGHT at Missouri Bottom Rd, 4 lane road, crossover I-270 for left turn lane
LEFT on Mo. Hwy 370 (115) and follow to Discovery Bridge which crosses Missouri River to St. Charles.
Exit Mo. Hwy 370 for Missouri Bottom Rd
LEFT on Earth City Expressway

LEFT on St. Charles Rock Road
LEFT at Taussig Road
Straight at Mo. Hwy 370 overpass and follow Missouri Bottom Rd past I-270
LEFT on Fee Fee Road
RIGHT on McDonnell Blvd, across Lindbergh Blvd
LEFT at Eva Avenue
RIGHT at Frost Avenue and across 3 railroad tracks
LEFT at stop sign onto Hazelwood Blvd
RIGHT on Pershall and back to starting point

> OPTION to ride over Missouri River to St. Charles. Planned KATY Trail access after crossing bridge.

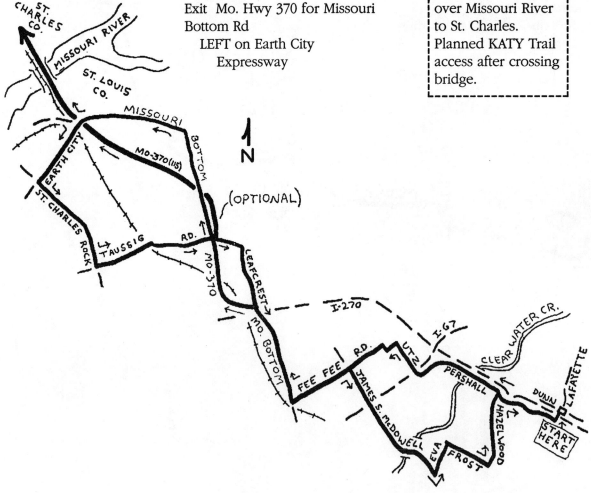

A SUNDAY MORNING 20-MILER

Starting Point: I-270, the intersection of Lafayette St. and Dunn Rd.
Distance: 20 miles
Approximate Pedaling Time: 1.5 Hours
Terrain: Gently rolling
Things To See: A suburban ride contributed by Ted Meyer. A great view from Sunset Park.

Starting from the intersection of Lafayette St. and Dunn Rd., cycle west on Dunn Rd.

crossing under Lindbergh Blvd.
RIGHT on Utz
RIGHT on Howdershell Rd/Shackleford Rd, a four and two lane road with road hazards and narrow shoulders
(option)LEFT at Sunset Park Road for a "great" hill returning from the lower picnic area Or continue north on Shackleford Road
Straight on Old Halls Ferry Road across New Halls Ferry Road
RIGHT at Vaile Rd

LEFT at New Halls Ferry rd
RIGHT into Wedgewood sub-division on Wedgewood Drive
LEFT at Wellington Drive
RIGHT at Indiancup Drive
RIGHT at Cottontail Drive
LEFT at Waterford Drive crossing Lindbergh Blvd.
RIGHT at stop sign for Waterford Drive
RIGHT on St. Anthony Lane
LEFT on Lafayette St and return to Dunn Rd

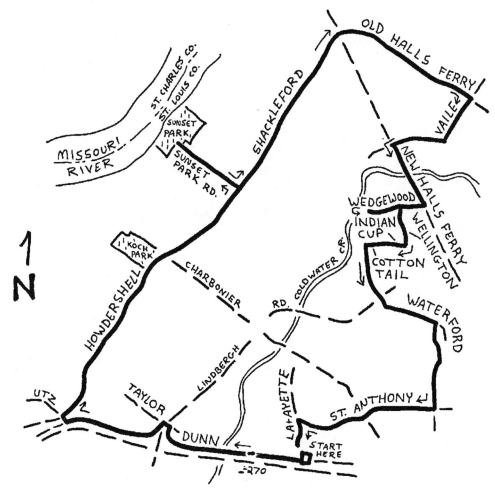

NORTH COUNTY LOOP

Starting Point: Bridgeton Athletic Complex
Distance: 47 miles
Approximate Pedaling Time: 3.5-4 hours
Terrain: Moderately hilly
Things To See: This is a popular ride in urban North St. Louis county

LEFT on Ferguson
LEFT on Taussig Rd
RIGHT at Missouri Bottom Rd
LEFT at Leaf Crest(top of hill)
LEFT on Dunn Rd
LEFT on Howdershell (expect heavy traffic) becomes Shackleford

LEFT on Shackleford one block past New Halls Ferry
Straight on Old Jamestown (same as Shackleford)
LEFT at Vail
RIGHT at Old Jamestown
LEFT on Parker Rd
LEFT on Bellefontaine
RIGHT at Spanish Pond bedcomes Strodtman, then Columbia Bottom Rd
RIGHT at Dunn Rd (just before I-270)
LEFT on Lilac
RIGHT on Shepley
LEFT at Bellefontaine
RIGHT at Chambers Rd (expect heavy traffic)

RIGHT on Elizabeth, cross over I-270
Continue straight on Washington (same as Elizabeth)
Washington becomes Charbonier when crossing Lindbergh
Charbonier becomes Aubuchon which becomes Missouri Bottom
LEFT on Missouri Bottom Rd
RIGHT at Taussig
LEFT at Ferguson into Bridgeton Athletic Complex

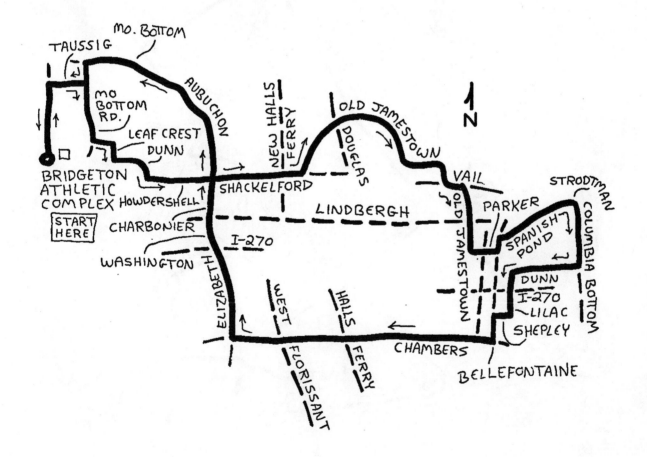

26

A TUESDAY RIDE TO FOREST PARK

Starting Point: Plaza Frontenac Shopping Center, Clayton and Lindbergh
Distance: 21 miles
Approximate Pedaling Time: 2 to 2.5 hours
Terrain: Moderately hilly
Things to See: Very urban cycling through Ladue, University City, and Clayton with a loop around Forest Park.

This is an organized ride on Tuesday morning lead by Sue Wilhelm. Not advisable for the novice cyclist. The traffic is heavy. The group is generally large, diverse, and friendly. Cycle north from the shopping center south parking lot.
LEFT on Clayton Rd.
RIGHT on Spoede and travel almost 2.0 miles
RIGHT at Ladue across Lindbergh for 2.6 miles
LEFT at Price
RIGHT on Delmar crossing Skinker and at about 4.5 miles
RIGHT on De Bauviere past Lindell into Forest Park
Continue on the marked bike path clockwise around the Park exiting on Forsythe
LEFT on Skinker

RIGHT at S. Rosebury
LEFT at Demun
RIGHT on San Bonita
LEFT on Big Bend
RIGHT at Dale
LEFT at Laclede Station
RIGHT on Folk
LEFT on Hanley
RIGHT at Litzsinger
LEFT at Eulalie which becomes Litzsinger at Brentwood Blvd.
Follow Litzsinger west
RIGHT after passing the Shriner's Hospital to the Plaza Frontenac Shopping Center.

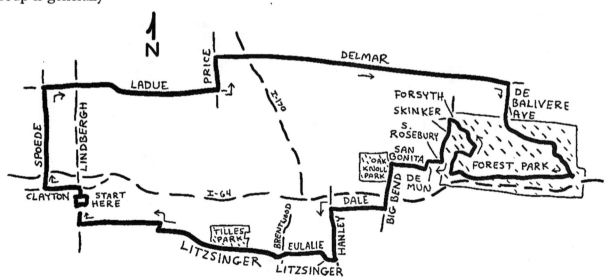

TWO PARKS AND A RIVER RIDE

Starting Point: Kirkwood Park, W. Adams & Geyer Rd
Distance: 35 miles
Approximate Pedaling Time: 3.5 hours
Terrain: Hilly
Things To See: A blend of urban and suburban. Valley Park, the Meramec River, and Castlewood Park. A stop for food at a White Castle.

A ride contributed by Bob Alsobrook.
Cycle west on W. Adams from Geyer Rd
LEFT on Couch
RIGHT on Big Bend
LEFT at Marshall Rd which features a 2 mile hill after crossing I-270
RIGHT at Meramec Station in Valley Park
LEFT on Vance Rd
RIGHT on Sulphur Springs
LEFT at Oak
LEFT at Ries Rd
LEFT at Kiefer Creek in Castlewood Park
Return by cycling west on Kiefer Creek

RIGHT on Ries Rd
RIGHT on Oak which becomes Big Bend at Sulphur Springs
LEFT at Hanna
RIGHT at Meramec Station - if you've reached Manchester, you've gone too far
LEFT on Carman and stay left at fork about 3 miles called Doughtery Ferry
LEFT on Barrett Station
LEFT at Manchester Rd to White Castle
RIGHT on Mason Rd
RIGHT on Claayton Rd across I-270
RIGHT at Geyer Rd to the starting point

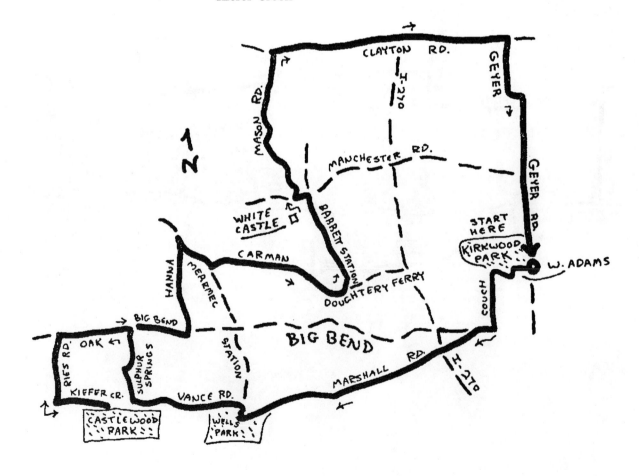

28

KIRKWOOD TO SUSON PARK

Starting Point: Kirkwood Community Center,
Adams Ave & Geyer Rd
Distance: 28 miles
Approximate Pedaling Time: 2-2.5 hours
Terrain: Mostly flat
Things To See: An urban out and back ride.

Cycle south on Geyer Rd crossing Big Bend, I-44, and Watson
RIGHT on Rott Rd
LEFT jog on Robyn Rd
RIGHT again on Rott Rd.
LEFT at Weber Hill Rd which becomes Kennerly when crossing Gravois
LEFT after crossing Tesson Ferry on Old Tesson
RIGHT at Mattis Rd
RIGHT on Ambs Rd
LEFT on Butler Hill
RIGHT at Kerth Rd with a right and left jog
RIGHT at Meramec Bottoms
RIGHT on Wells
LEFT into Suson Park

Return by the same route.

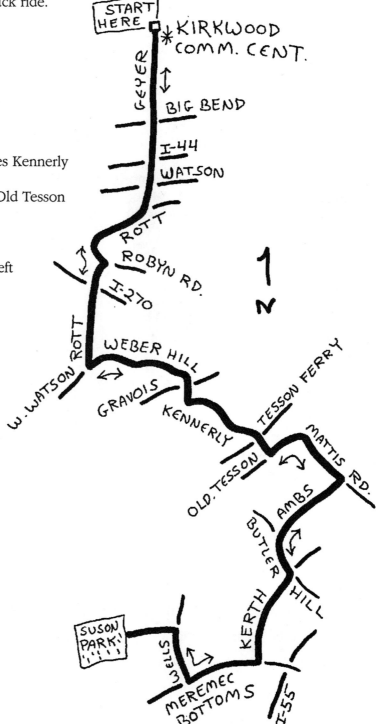

CENTRAL WEST END FOR BREAKFAST

Starting Point: Kirkwood Community Center, Geyer & Adams
Distance: 40 miles
Approximate Pedaling Time: 3.5-4 hours
Terrain: Flat city route
Things To See: "This is a fun city route, but ride with caution" says Jim Jeske. Don't miss a stop at the St. Louis Bread Company at Maryland & Euclid.

Cycle from the Kirkwood Community Center west on Adams which feeds into Ballas Rd
LEFT at Dougherty Ferry
RIGHT at Barrett Station (go around gate)
RIGHT on Thornhill
LEFT on Topping
LEFT at Clayton
RIGHT at Mason
RIGHT on Conway

RIGHT on Spoede
LEFT at Clayton
RIGHT at S 40
RIGHT on Rolling Rock Ln
RIGHT on Roan Ln
LEFT at Daniel
LEFT at Litzinger
LEFT on High School
Continue on McCutcheon
RIGHT at Clayton
LEFT at Hanley
RIGHT on Wydowne
LEFT on Skinker
RIGHT into Forest Park to pick up bike path, or
RIGHT at Lindell
RIGHT at Park Rd (before Kingshighway) becomes W. Pine
(LEFT at Euclid for 2 blocks for the St. Louis bread Co; bagels at the corner of W. Pine & Euclid)
RIGHT on Taylor
LEFT on Manchester

RIGHT at Tower Grove
RIGHT at Magnolia
LEFT on Kingshighway - immediate right, and right again
LEFT on Columbia
RIGHT at Southwest
LEFT at January
RIGHT on Arsenal
LEFT on Watson
RIGHT at Flyler which becomes McCausland
RIGHT at Landsdowne
LEFT at Murdock (cut-off) crossing Laclede Station and I-44
LEFT on Big Bend
RIGHT on Lockwood
LEFT at Berry
RIGHT becoming Adams
LEFT at Geyer to the Kirkwood Community Center

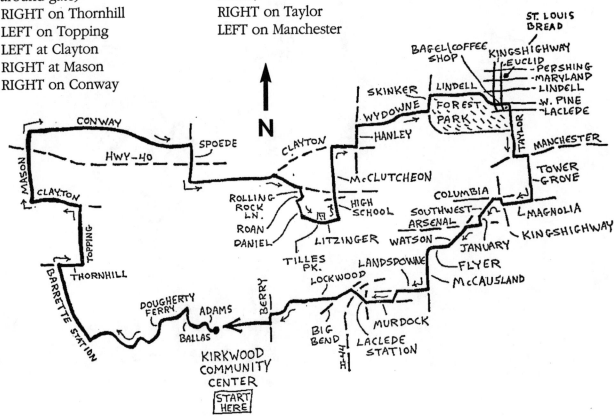

MASTODON STATE PARK RIDE

Starting Point: St. Anthony's Hospital, I-270 & Tesson Ferry Rd (Hwy 21)
Distance: Approx. 40 miles
Approximate Pedaling Time: 3-3.5 hours
Terrain: Moderately hilly
Things To See: This Jefferson County ride is a favorite of Jim Klages. It's mostly two lane roads with a blend of suburban and rural. The turn-around point is Mastodon State Park and a short distance south is the population center of the U.S.

Starting from the intersection of I-270 and Tesson Ferry Rd, cycle south on Tesson Ferry (Hwy 21) across the Meramec River

RIGHT on Hwy 141
LEFT at stop light (Spring Dale Park pool on right)
RIGHT at Schneider Dr
LEFT on E. Romaine Creek and a tough hill
LEFT on West Rock Creek crossing Hwy 21 becoming East Rock Creek and winding southeasterly
RIGHT at Old Lemay Ferry Rd
LEFT at Seckman Rd with Seckman Jr. High on right
Seckman Rd continues through Mastodon State Park to I-55 where you turnaround for the return trip.

31

HOUSE SPRINGS LOOP

Starting Point: WAL-MART in South County on Old Hwy 30
Distance: 1st loop 25 Miles; 2nd loop 19 Miles
Approximate Pedaling Time: 1st loop 2 Hours; 2nd loop 1.5 hours
Terrain: Very hilly
Things To See: A Jefferson County ride that's very rural and especially beautiful in spring, says Bob Alsobrook.

Cycle from Wal-Mart south on Old Hwy 30 staying to right at Hardees
RIGHT on W
LEFT on Byrnesville Rd
LEFT at NN
LEFT at Cedar Hill
RIGHT on Graham Rd
LEFT on Dulin Creek Rd with stop at Hardees' after first loop
Cycle left (west) on W

LEFT at Lower Byrnesville
LEFT at Old Hwy 30
RIGHT (south) on Hillsboro Local Road
LEFT at fork remaining on Hillsboro Local Rd
LEFT on Dulin Creek Rd back to Wal-Mart

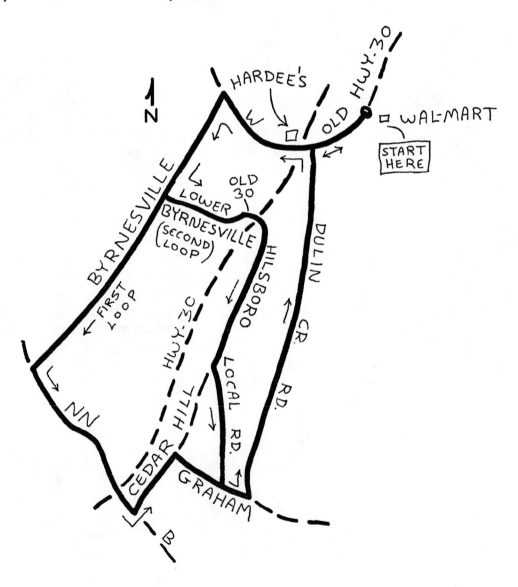

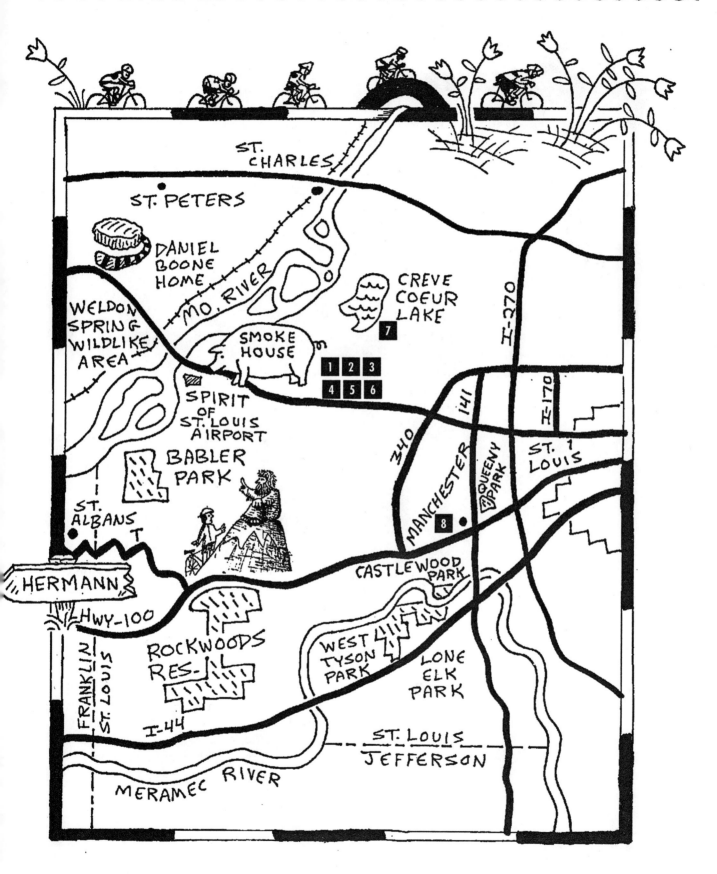

ST. CHARLES

ST. PETERS

DANIEL BOONE HOME

WELDON SPRING WILDLIKE AREA

MO. RIVER

CREVE COEUR LAKE

I-270

SMOKE HOUSE

7

1 **2** **3**
4 **5** **6**

SPIRIT OF ST. LOUIS AIRPORT

141

I-170

340

MANCHESTER

QUEENY PARK

ST. LOUIS 1

BABLER PARK

ST. ALBANS

8

HERMANN

CASTLEWOOD PARK

HWY-100

ROCKWOODS RES.

WEST TYSON PARK

LONE ELK PARK

FRANKLIN ST. LOUIS

I-44

ST. LOUIS JEFFERSON

MERAMEC RIVER

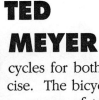

TED MEYER

cycles for both relaxation and exercise. The bicycle became his primary means of transportation for two years after joining the Air Force and Ted utilized a bicycle whenever possible for sixteen years of his military career. Since retiring, Ted has increased his annual mileage substantially. He attributes this to riding with groups where the miles seem to go by faster and easier. His choice of groups are Missouri Meanders and the St. Louis Bicycle Touring Society. Ted also prefers the challenge of city and urban riding but also appreciates the wide open spaces of the country rides. His hopes for the future include the completion of the St. Louis Riverfront Bike Path and the connection of the KATY Trail over the Mississippi River at Alton.

JULIE WYNN

moved to St. Louis in 1987 and knew that she wanted to try bicycling, but didn't know where to begin. Thanks to the help of warm and friendly area cyclists, she gathered information, purchased a bike, and the rest is history. After three years of recreational touring all over the country, she started her own bicycle touring company, Missouri Meanders. Her love is to take people to her favorite places and help them see the countryside from the seat of a bicycle. She is always happy to talk with and encourage beginners to learn the joys of bicycling.

IT HAS ITS UPS AND DOWNS

Starting Point: Smokehouse Restaurant, Chesterfield
Distance: 54 Miles
Approximate Pedaling Time: 4-5 Hours
Terrain: Very hilly
Things To See: The incredible hills of West County; Mae's Restaurant in St. Albans; Babler Park; pig out after the ride at The Smokehouse.

This tough ride is the work of Bob Alsobrook. The area around Chesterfield was badly hurt by the flood but should be ready for the 1994 season. The area around St. Albans is being rapidly developed so enjoy it now.

Cycle west on Chesterfield Airport Rd
LEFT on Olive St. Rd
LEFT on Eatherton Rd which turns into Hwy C
RIGHT at Hwy 109, watch for sewer grates

RIGHT into Babler State Park and circle right
LEFT on Hwy 109 upon exiting park and again watch for sewer grates
RIGHT at Hwy C
LEFT at Eatherton Rd
RIGHT on Orville Rd and steep hill
RIGHT on Shepard Rd
LEFT at Hwy 109 - go past Hwy 100 & Manchester Rd
RIGHT at Woods
LEFT on Melrose
RIGHT on Hwy 100
LEFT at Melrose
RIGHT at Ossenfort
LEFT on Hwy T
RIGHT on St. Albans Rd (back entrance)
LEFT at Hwy T
RIGHT at Ossenfort
LEFT on Wild Horse Creek
LEFT on Eatherton
RIGHT at Olive St Rd
RIGHT at Chesterfield Airport Rd to Smokehouse and a just reward

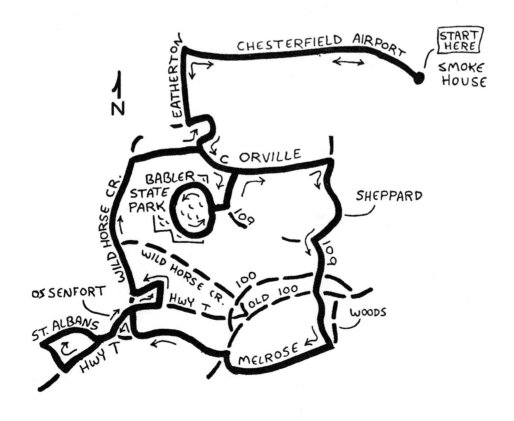

WORK UP AN APPETITE

Starting Point: The Smoke House on Chesterfield Airport Rd
Distance: 65 Miles
Approximate Pedaling Time: 4-5 Hours
Terrain: Very hilly
Things To See: When veteran cyclist Bob Alsobrook says, "very hilly," expect a challenge. But, keep in mind, "hills are only flats at an angle" and "the only way to eat an elephant is one bite at a time". Food and drink at Mae's in St. Albans and at The Smoke House in Chesterfield at the end of the ride.

Cycle east from the Smoke House on Chesterfield Airport Rd
RIGHT on Baxter Rd on west side of Chesterfield Mall
RIGHT on Clayton Rd
LEFT at Strecker
LEFT at Hwy 100(Manchester)for short distance
RIGHT on Old State Rd and bear hard right at Hwy 109 fork

LEFT on Woods
LEFT at Melrose which merges with Allenton Six-Flags crossing I-44
RIGHT at BR 44 (or Hwy 100) which becomes Hwy AT when crossing I-44
RIGHT on M heading north
RIGHT fork at former D. Sands Restaurant on Hwy T into St. Albans and good food at Mae's Restaurant
East on Ossenfort Rd
LEFT at fork on Wild Horse Rd
LEFT at Long which curves right becoming Chesterfield Airport Rd and the Smoke House.

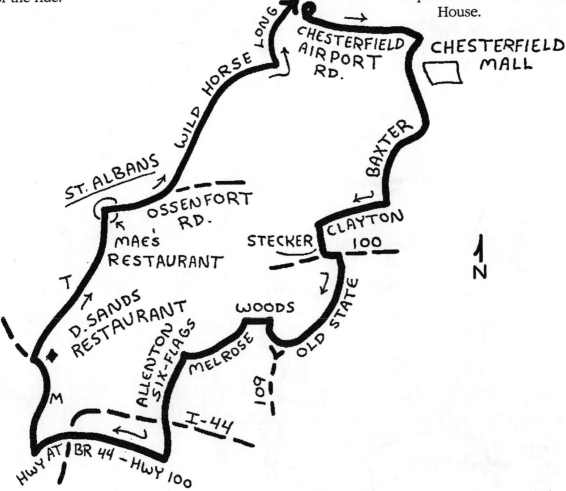

PACIFIC - THE HARD WAY

Starting Point: The Smoke House Restaurant on Chesterfield Airport Rd
Distance: 50 Miles
Approximate Pedaling Time: 4-4.5 Hours
Terrain: Very hilly
Things To See: Claus Claussen of The St. Louis Cycling Club says "hilly is beautiful" and this is a very beautiful ride. Hwy OO is "ooh ooh", Bouquet is quite hilly, and the highlight of the ride are the hills on the second half of the course.

Cycle from The Smoke House Restaurant south
RIGHT on Wild Horse Creek
LEFT on Kehrs Hill
RIGHT at Strecker
RIGHT into Sheppard
RIGHT at Hwy 109
LEFT on Pond
RIGHT on Rieger
LEFT at Wild Horse Creek
RIGHT at Hwy 100

RIGHT on Old Manchester for short ride and LEFT onto Hwy 100
LEFT on Allentown Rd with Ramada on left and 6 FLAGS on right
RIGHT on Business 44 into Pacific and McDonalds for food
RIGHT at Hwy OO for hills
RIGHT at Old Manchester
LEFT on Bouquet
RIGHT on Melrose
LEFT at Ossenfort curving to right crossing Hwy T
LEFT at Wild Horse Creek which turns right at "Doberman Hill" - you'll know how it got its name.
Follow Wild Horse Creek back to The Smoke House Restaurant

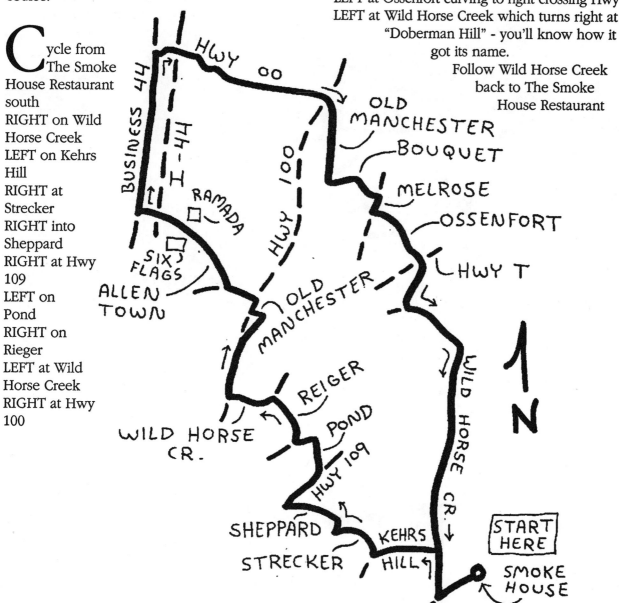

ST. ALBANS - THE HARD WAY

Starting Point: The Smoke House Restaurant in Chesterfield
Distance: 48 Miles
Approximate Pedaling Time:4-4.5 Hours
Terrain: Very hilly
Things To See: Lots and lots of hills, says Claus Claussen of The St. Louis Cycling Club. A welcome stop at 33 miles is Mae's Restaurant in St. Albans.

Cycle south from The Smoke House.
RIGHT on Wild Horse Creek
LEFT on Kehrs Hill

RIGHT at Strecker
RIGHT at Sheppard
RIGHT on Hwy 109 for short distance
LEFT on Pond Rd across Hwy 100
RIGHT at Old Manchester and left to Hwy 100
LEFT on 6 Flags-Allenton Rd with Ramada on right and 6 Flags on left

RIGHT on Fox Creek Rd, very hilly across Hwy 100 becoming Old Manchester Rd
RIGHT at Bassett Rd and more hills
LEFT at Hwy T and more hills
RIGHT first turn to St. Albans, Mae's Restauraant
Return to Hwy T east
LEFT at Hardt
LEFT across narrow bridge on Wild Horse Creek which winds its way back north to The Smoke House Restaurant

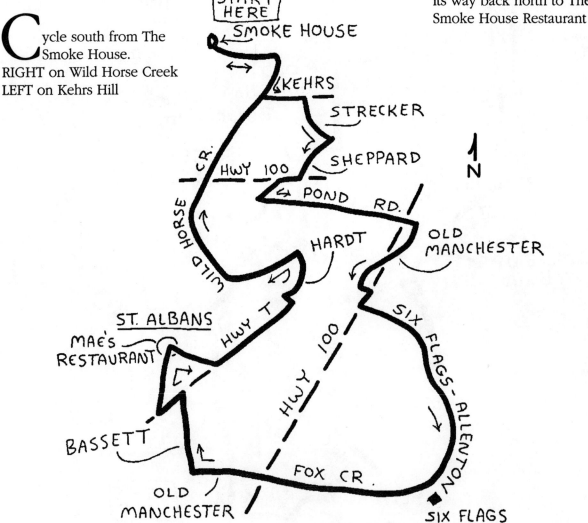

RIDE AROUND BABLER PARK

Starting Point: The Smoke House or West County YMCA
Distance: 34 Miles
Approximate Pedaling Time: 2.5-3 Hours
Terrain: Very hilly
Things To See: Lots of hills, Babler Park, and St. Albans. This ride was contributed by Paul Moskovitz.

Cycle west on Chesterfield Airport Rd past the airport and prison At gas station the road splits, continue west on Olive St past Rombach's pumpkin patch

LEFT at Eatherton Rd and single file
RIGHT at Centaur to avoid hills
LEFT across tracks on Centaur, watch out for dogs
RIGHT on Wild Horse Creek at T-intersection

RIGHT at fork on Ossenfort Rd where hills start
RIGHT at hilltop on Hwy T (also called New St. Albans Rd)

Sharp RIGHT at St. Albans Golf & Country Club
Return the same way

OPTION for hills and circuit of Babler Park
Continue south across tracks on Eatherton
RIGHT on Hwy CC
LEFT on Wild Horse Creek
LEFT at John Cochran into Babler Park
After some hill work in Babler Park exit north on John Cochran
LEFT on Wild Horse Creek and continue ride to St. Albans

RIDE TO ROCKWOOD RESERVATION

Starting Point: The Smoke House in Chesterfield
Terrain: Very hilly
Things To See: Another challenging ride by Paul Moskovitz. Sights include Babler Park, Rockwood Reservation, and Greensfelder Park with its equestrian and hiking trails.

Cycle west on Chesterfield Airport Rd past the airport and prison. The road splits at the gas station, continue west on Olive St past Rombach's pumpkin patch
LEFT at Eatherton Rd and cycle single file
LEFT across tracks on Centaur, watch out for dogs
RIGHT on Wild Horse Creek at T-intersection
LEFT on Hwy T across Hwy 100
LEFT at Manchester
RIGHT at Glencoe into Rockwood Reservation, a very picturesque ride
RIGHT on Melrose up big hill for scenic view of Rockwood Reservation

Continue Melrose west out of Rockwood Reservation,
Stay on Melrose west across Allenton-Six Flags Rd
RIGHT at Hwy 100
LEFT at first turn intersection of Woodland Meadows Rd and Manchester Rd
LEFT again on Melrose Rd

RIGHT on Ossenfort Rd which becomes Wild Horse Creek Rd
LEFT at Centaur Rd
RIGHT after railroad tracks still on Centaur Rd
LEFT at Centaur and follow Eatherton and Olive St Rd back to Chesterfield

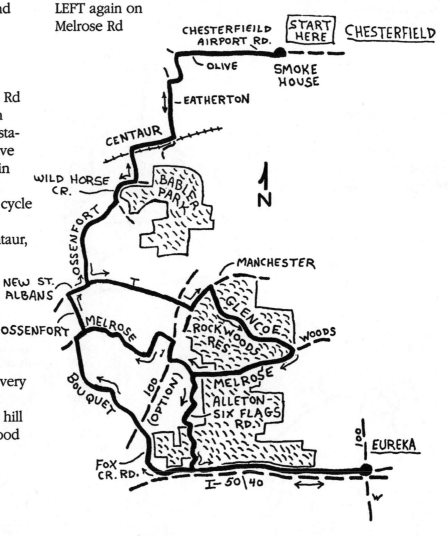

OPTION to Greensfelder Park
LEFT on Allenton-Six Flags Rd
LEFT on West 5th into Eureka for food
RIGHT (west) on West 5th
RIGHT at Fox Creek Rd, very pretty
LEFT at Hwy 100 onto Old Manchester Rd

RIGHT on Bouquet
RIGHT on Melrose
LEFT at Ossenfort Rd, heading north to Wild Horse Creek and same route as other riders back to Chesterfield

BALLWIN TO ST. ALBANS

Starting Point: Central Plaza Shopping Center, Manchester Rd & New Ballwin
Distance: 43 Miles
Approximate Pedaling Time: 3.5-4 Hours
Terrain: Hilly
Things To See: Rockwood Reservation and St. Albans

This interesting and challenging out and back route is the work of Bob Alsobrook.

Cycle south from Central Plaza Shopping Center on New Ballwin
RIGHT at Kiefer Creek
LEFT at St. Paul which curves to the right
RIGHT on Ridge Rd
LEFT on Old State Rd
RIGHT at Hwy 109 intersection across Woods into Rockwood Reservation
Continue on Glencoe Rd through Rockwood
LEFT on Old Manchester for short distance
RIGHT on Hwy T crossing Hwy 100, Ossenfort Rd into St. Albans for food at Mae's
Exit St. Albans cycling east on St. Albans Rd which merges into Hwy T
Return the same route traveling east to the starting point.

MISSOURI RIVER VALLEY RIDE

Starting Point: Creve Coeur Park
Distance: 24 miles
Approximate Pedaling Time: 1.5-2 hours
Terrain: Mostly flat
Things To See: This is a personal favorite of Tom Yarbrough (SLBTS). It's a weekday morning ride along the Missouri River.

Cycle north from Creve Coeur on Marine
LEFT on Creve Coeur Mill (heavy traffic)
RIGHT on River Valley and stay left
RIGHT at Riverbend
RIGHT at Olive
RIGHT on Hog Hollow which becomes River Valley
LEFT on Creve Coeur
RIGHT at Marine back to Creve Coeur Park

OPTION:
continue 2 miles
into Faust Park

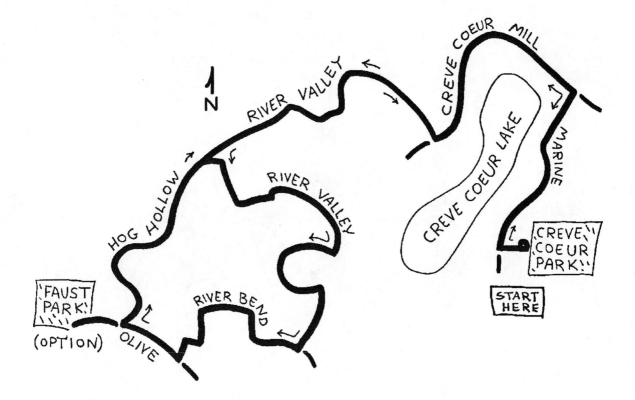

ARE YOU IN SHAPE?

Starting Point:
Glencoe Rd in
Rockwoods
Reservation, from either
I-44 or Hwy 100
Distance: 50 Miles
**Approximate
Pedaling Time:** 4-4.5
Hours
Terrain: Very hilly
Things To See: The
name says it all. This is
another ride con-
tributed by Bob
Alsobrook who says it's
challenging.

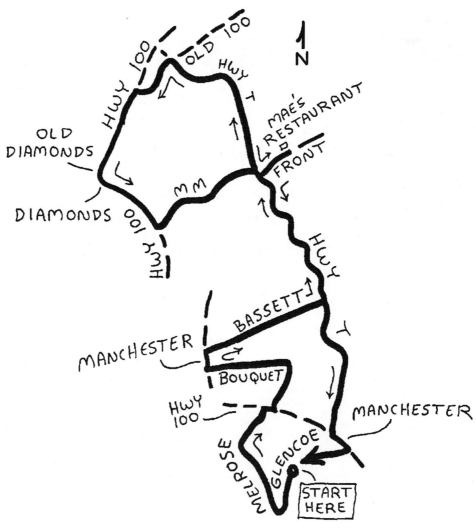

Cycle southeast on Glencoe Rd
RIGHT on Melrose
RIGHT at Hwy 100
LEFT at Bouquet
RIGHT on Manchester Rd
RIGHT on Bassett Rd
LEFT at Hwy T known for its hills
LEFT at Old Hwy 100
LEFT on Hwy 100
LEFT on Hwy at Old Diamonds
LEFT at Hwy 100 at New Diamonds
LEFT at MM
RIGHT on Hwy T
LEFT on Front St to Mae's Restaurant
LEFT at Hwy T
LEFT on Manchester Rd
RIGHT on Glencoe to Rockwoods Reservation starting point

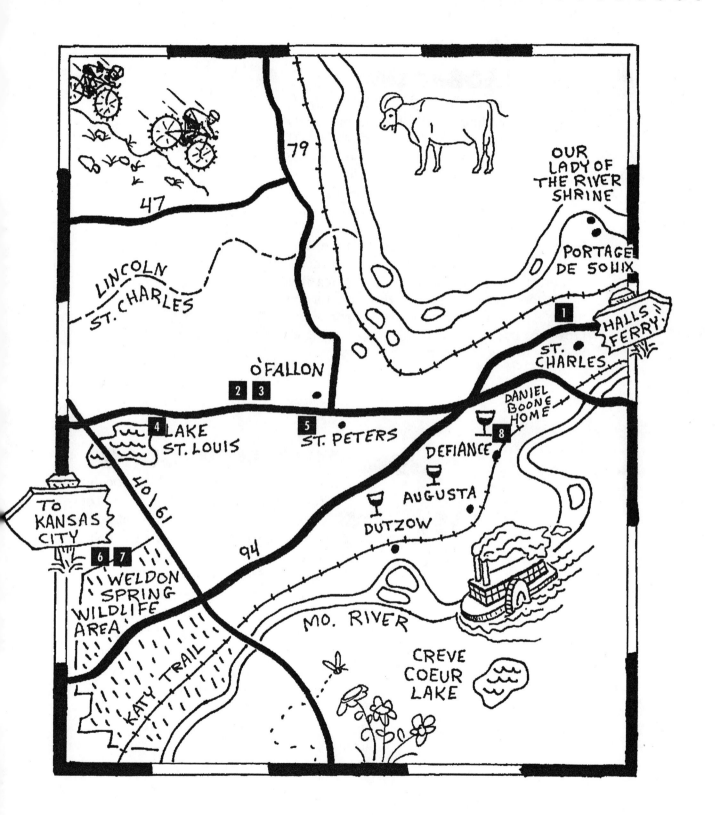

47

BOB ALSOBROOK

began cycling in 1985 when he found an outdoor activity he and his family could enjoy together. Bob joined AYH because of a large and diverse schedule of rides. He rode the rides led by Natalie Kekeisen who recognized Bob's leadership quality and cycling ability and asked him to become a ride leader. From '87 through '93, Bob led the AYH Tuesday morning ride. There's probably not a significant ride in the entire St. Louis area that Bob Alsobrook hasn't ridden. His hope for the future is "that cycling popularity continues to grow because it seems that motorists treat us better as we become more visible."

TOM YARBROUGH

combines his work with his avocation. Tom is executive director of The St. Louis Bicycle Touring Society. His interest in cycling began in 1972 when, as a college student, he depended upon a bicycle as transportation. In 1976 Tom Yarbrough joined the Touring Cyclist and a year later became a store manager. In 1978 Tom organized the Touring Cyclist' first tour, a ride to Hermann, MO. The Touring Society (SLBTS) was born a year later and Tom began building a reputation yet unmatched for first class, quality rides. Tom is also a board member of Gateway Trailnet, which reflects his total commitment to making the St. Louis area the finest possible place to cycle.

MUELLER FIELD MONDAY NITE RIDE

Starting Point: Mueller Soccer Field, north of Old St. Charles & west of Hwy 94

Distance: 17 miles with an extra 8 mile loop

Approximate Pedaling Time: 1-1.5 hours

Terrain: Flat and fast

Things To See: River bottom land; food and drink after the ride.

This is a Monday evening Touring Society ride. It's an opportunity to loosen up after a tough weekend ride or to try out some new equipment. There should be some award for anyone who finds anything like a hill on the route. It's a sentimental favorite because it was my inaugural St. Louis bike ride.

From Mueller Sports Complex cycle left (northwest) on Mueller Rd
RIGHT on Airport-Crittenden Lane
LEFT at T-intersection which is Hwy B

RIGHT at fork on Washeon Rd
RIGHT on Orchard Rd
At four-way, Orchard becomes Hwy V, continue straight east
Turn around at Hwy 94 intersection with Orchard Farm school on north side and return
the same way.

8-Mile Loop option

LEFT on Hwy 94
LEFT on Grafton Ferry Rd
RIGHT at Portage Rd which takes you around the airport
RIGHT at Rees Rd
RIGHT on Hwy 94
RIGHT on Hwy V at Orchard Farm School

FORT ZUMWALT TO WRIGHT CITY

Starting Point: Ft. Zumwalt State Park entrance, southwest of O'Fallon, MO
Distance: 42 miles
Approximate Pedaling Time: 3 hours
Terrain: Rolling
Things To See: Rural countryside with food in Wright City.

Cycle west from church on Hwy 175 across from entrance to Ft. Zumwalt State Park
LEFT on Bryan
RIGHT on Feise
LEFT at Hanley
RIGHT on N across Z and T
N becomes OO
RIGHT on M
RIGHT on F into Wright City

RETURN the same way.

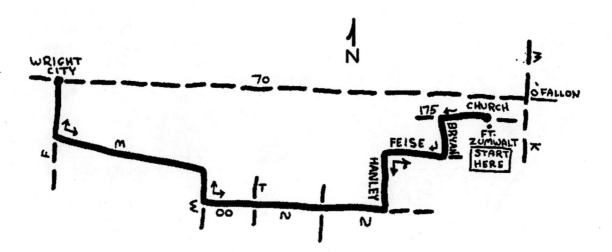

PASSPORT TO MOSCOW

Starting Point: O'Fallon, MO Civic Park north of railroad tracks & west of Main St.
Distance: 40 Miles
Approximate Pedaling Time: 4 Hours
Terrain: Rolling
Things To See: Picturesque bridge over Cuiver River. Stop for food at Betty's Country Kafe in Moscow Mills

A ride contributed by Bob Alsobrook.
Cycle east from Civic Park in O'Fallon
LEFT on Main St
LEFT on P
RIGHT at St. Paul
RIGHT with church on left and continue north on St. Paul

LEFT at Y which meanders north across Cuiver River
Gravel road for short way after bridge
LEFT at Hwy OO
LEFT on C into Moscow Mills

Return to O'Fallon by the same route.

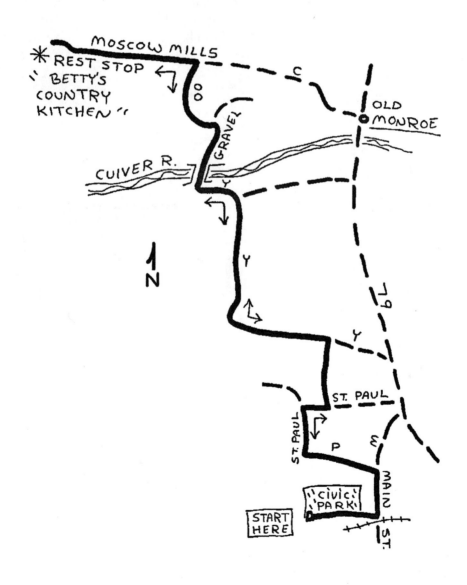

RIDE TO DOG PRAIRIE TAVERN

Starting Point: Lake St. Louis exit I-70
Distance: 22 miles + 16 extra miles
Approximate Pedaling Time: 2 hours + 1 hour for extra loop
Terrain: Moderately hilly
Things To See: This is a very popular scenic ride along Cuivre River; Food at Dog Prairie Tavern and in Old Monroe.

Cycle from Lake St. Louis Park under I-70 and left on access road
RIGHT on Josephville Rd with GM plant on left
Becomes Eisenbath after Josephville, stay right
LEFT on Freymuth
OPTION:
LEFT on Hwy Y
LEFT at Cuivre River
RIGHT across bridge and 1/4 mile gravel
Tavern at Chain of Rocks
Continue on scenic Hwy OO

RIGHT on Hwy C north to Old Monroe
RIGHT at Old Hwy 79 across Cuivre River
RIGHT at Dyer Rd
RIGHT on Flatwoods Rd
LEFT on Hwy Y

Continue north on Hwy Y
RIGHT at St. Paul Rd and Dog Prairie Tavern
RIGHT at Church
LEFT on Freymuth which becomes Gutherie
RIGHT on Hancock
RIGHT at Mexico
LEFT at access road to Lake St. Louis Park

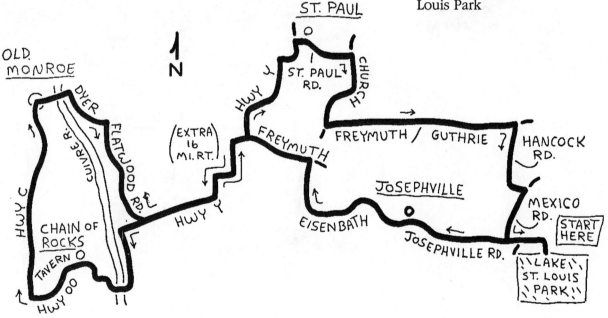

TAKE THE FERRY BOAT TOUR

Starting Point: St. Peters Commuter Parking Lot, St. Peters, MO off I-70
Distance: 72 or 106 miles
Approximate Pedaling Time: 6 or 8 hours
Terrain: Mostly flat, two-lane blacktop roads
Things To See: Good food available in Brussels, Hardin, and Pere Marquette State Park. After lunch at Royce's Restaurant in Hardin, decide whether or not you're up to 34 extra miles. Choice of 3 or 4 ferry rides. This ride contributed by Jim Jeske traverses four counties.

LEFT from commuter parking lot in St. Peters
Continue through Old Town St. Peters
City St. turns into Hwy C after tracks
RIGHT on Hwy B
LEFT on Golden Ferry Rd (one mile gravel)
CROSS Mississippi River on Golden Eagle (Toll Ferry)
RIGHT at first stop sign (no road sign)
LEFT at second stop sign (no road sign)
LEFT end of road (stop sign but no road sign)
Continue on main road through Brussels to Hardin
LEFT at stop sign in middle of Hardin
RIGHT side of street after 2 blocks is Royce's Restaurant
Decide on 72 mile or 106 mile route before leaving Hardin

RIGHT on Hwy 100
CONTINUE past Pere Marquette Park (water & rest rooms)
RIGHT on Brussels Ferry (free)
CROSS Illinois River on Brussels Ferry
LEFT at road to Golden Eagle Ferry (no road sign)
RIGHT at first stop sign (no roadsign)

> **106 Mile Four Ferry Ride**
> CONTINUE through Hardin after lunch
> Strait at the bridge in Hardin; North on Hwy 100
> LEFT at Hamburg Road just before Michael (no sign)
> STAY RIGHT when you come to Hamburg (no street signs)
> RIGHT at end of Hamburg road. Road along river.
> RIGHT at Hwy 96
> LEFT Hwy 100 the end of Hwy 96 in Kampsville
> RIGHT at Kampsville on Hwy 108

> **72 Mile Three Ferry Route**
> After lunch return to stop sign and turn left
> RIGHT on Hwy 16/100
> CROSS BRIDGE over Illinois River

LEFT at second stop sign (no road sign)
CROSS Mississippi River on Golden Eagle Ferry (toll)
RIGHT on Hwy B (end of gravel road)
LEFT on Hwy C (end of Hwy B)
CONTINUE through Old Town St. Peters to parking lot
RIGHT into commuter parking lot

> CROSS Illinois River on Kampsville Ferry (free)
> RIGHT on Eldred Rd in Eldred (sign difficult to find)
> LEFT at end of Eldred Rd onto Hwy 16/100 (no sign)

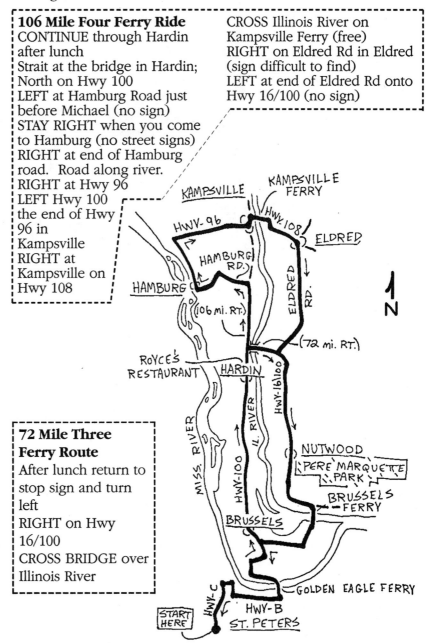

DANIEL BOONE'S PLACE

Starting Point: Busch Wildlife
Distance: 35 Miles
Approximate Pedaling Time: 3-3.5 Hours
Terrain: Moderately hilly
Things To See: Bob Alsobrook calls this ride "very rural". Sites include Daniel Boone home, a picturesque old church in Femme Osage, and New Melle

Cycle South from Busch Wildlife
RIGHT on D
LEFT at DD
RIGHT at F and look for Daniel Boone's home on left
LEFT on Femme Osage Rd into Femme Osage
RIGHT on T
RIGHT at D past New Melle and back to Busch Wildlife

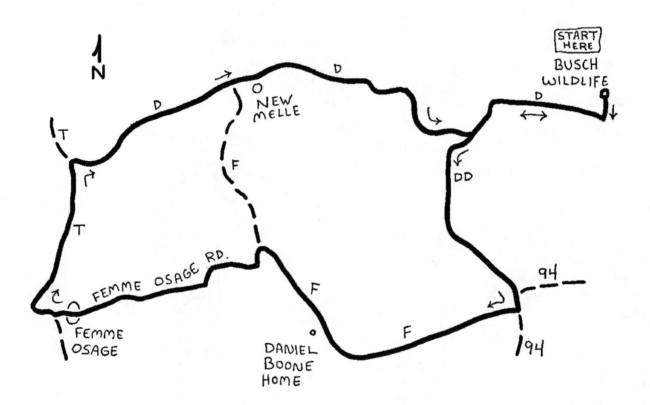

FOR HILL LOVERS

Starting Point: Busch Wildlife, Weldon Springs
Distance: 75 Miles
Approximate Pedaling Time:5+ Hours
Terrain: Hilly
Things To See: Claus Claussen of The St. Louis Cycling Club says this ride is for "hill lovers". In summer and fall, ride early to avoid traffic. The valley is beautiful; Augusta has a winery and Dutzow features shops and restaurants. Femme Osage has a historic church and cemetery. And, if your legs are feeling okay, try the Daniel Boone home. For the cyclist tired of the flat terrain of the KATY Trail, try this ride for its hills along Hwy 94 to the north.

Cycle east from Busch Wildlife
RIGHT on Hwy 94 thru Defiance.
Continue on Hwy 94 up Klondike Hill for 10 miles of hills from August to Dutzow.
Left (south) from Dutzow and RIGHT on Hwy 94/47 thru Marthasville
RIGHT to Treloar and Jan's Restaurant
North on Hwy 94 thru Hostein
RIGHT at Hwy 47 to Marthasville

LEFT (north) on Hwy D and hills
RIGHT on Hwy T to Femme Osage
LEFT on Femme Osage Rd
RIGHT at Hwy F past Daniel Boone's home
LEFT at Hwy DD where it intersects with Hwy 94
RIGHT into Busch Wildlife and the starting point.

DANIEL BOONE REVISITED

Starting Point: On Hwy F after exiting Hwy 94, southwest of Weldon Spring Wildlife
Distance: 21 Miles & 7 extra miles
Approximate Pedaling Time: 2.5-3 hours
Terrain:3 major hills and the rest easy
Things To See: Daniel Boone home and cafe, wineries at Augusta and Dutzow

Cycle left (north) from Daniel Boone home
LEFT at Femme Osage Creek Rd
OPTION at Femme Osage
Short tour riders LEFT on Hwy T to Augusta
Longer riders RIGHT on Hwy T
LEFT on Hwy TT to Dutzow
LEFT on Hwy 94
RIGHT at Emke Rd
LEFT at

Augusta Bottom Rd to Augusta

All riders continue on Hwy 94
LEFT at Schluersburg Rd for monster up hill, then downhill with narrow bridge
LEFT on Hwy F to Daniel Boone home

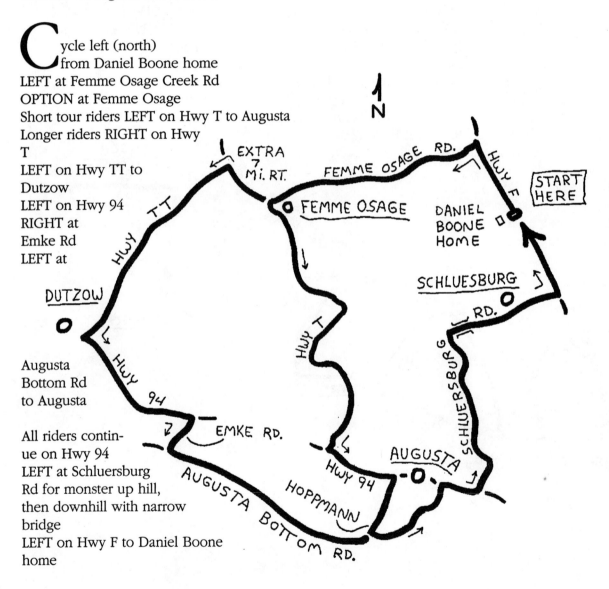

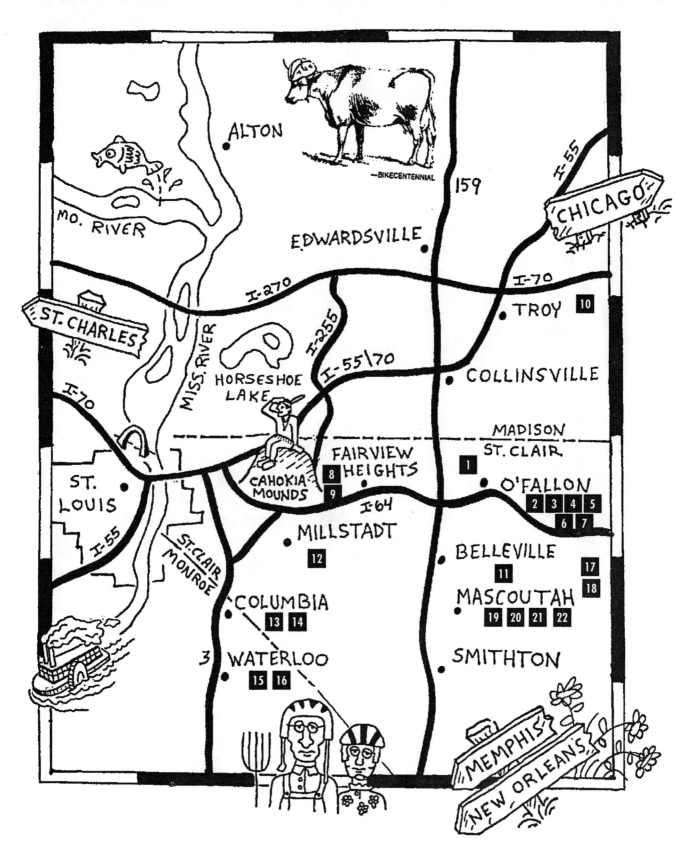

ALTON

—BIKECENTENNIAL

MO. RIVER

EDWARDSVILLE

159

I-55

CHICAGO

I-270

I-70

TROY 10

ST. CHARLES

MISS. RIVER

I-355

I-55\70

COLLINSVILLE

HORSESHOE LAKE

MADISON
ST. CLAIR

FAIRVIEW HEIGHTS

1

I-70

CAHOKIA MOUNDS

8
9

O'FALLON

2 3 4 5

ST. LOUIS

6 7

I-64

MILLSTADT

BELLEVILLE

I-55

ST. CLAIR
MONROE

12

11

17
18

MASCOUTAH

COLUMBIA

19 20 21 22

13 14

3 WATERLOO

15 16

SMITHTON

MEMPHIS
NEW ORLEANS

DAVE WEIDLER

began cycling in 1972 when prompted by a classmate bought an Italian bicycle. Ten years later, Dave traded up again, and joined companions, which led to organized rides. He rides the area around Mascoutah and St. Clair county. Dave rides with the Belleville Area Bicycling and Eating Society (BABES). He prefers touring to off-road cycling and when he finds a suitable replacement for his stoker, he'll enjoy his tandem once again.

RAY LATIMER

began cycling in 1987 with a local group on Wednesday evenings. He cycled about 1000 miles the first year, kept increasing his annual mileage, and completed a 24 day cross country tour in 1993. For group cycling, Ray prefers the Belleville Area Bicycling & Eating Society (BABES) and he generally cycles the area east of the Mississippi.

DAVE'S ANNUAL EASTER RIDE

Starting Point: Brinker's Restaurant, eact of Hwy 159 on Salem Rd north of O'Fallon
Distance: 36 miles
Approximate Pedaling Time: 3 hours
Terrain: Rolling hills
Things To See: This is Dave Weidler's annual Easter ride although you can take it anytime you wish. Dave says, "For some unknown reason people really like this ride." Let him know your reasons.

Cycle east on Salem Dr (N. Frontage Rd) where it intersects with Lincoln Trail at Glenview
Sharp LEFT (no sign)
RIGHT on Smiley Rd
LEFT on O'Fallon-Troy Rd north across County Line
RIGHT at Lebanon Rd
LEFT at Liberty Rd
LEFT on W. Mill Creek - watch for bad dogs!

RIGHT on Lockmann Rd
RIGHT at Lebanon Rd into Collinsville
LEFT at Blackjack
LEFT - hill(no sign)
RIGHT on Bethel Rd which becomes Bethel Meadows for a stretch

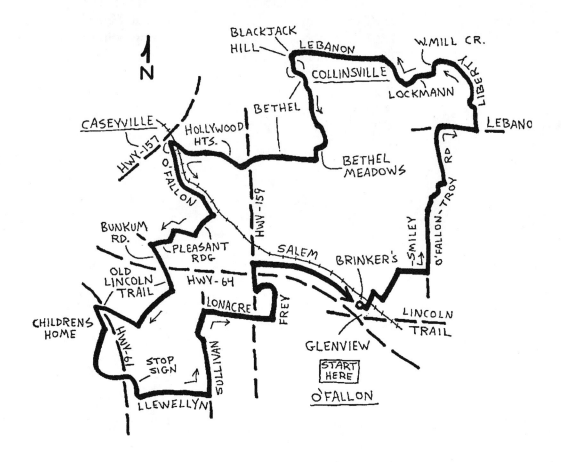

O'FALLON - CASEYVILLE LOOP

Starting Point: Schwinn Pedal-In, East Hwy 50, O'Fallon, IL.

Distance: 22 miles

Approximate Pedaling Time: 1.5 hours

Terrain: Moderately hilly with one medium grade

Things To See: Strawberry farm in E. O'Fallon open in mid-May and early June. The Dairy Haven in Caseyville is a welcome stop on a hot summer evening. An interesting collection of farmhouses along the way

This is an especially nice BABES ride for a summer evening when the Dairy Haven is open in Caseyville. Begin the ride by crossing East Hwy 50 in front of the Pedal-In Bike Shop and head north on Weber.

RIGHT at 1st St.

LEFT across railroad tracks on old wooden bridge.

LEFT on State St.

RIGHT at Smiley past school

LEFT at Wesley

RIGHT on N. Lincoln

LEFT on Smiley

LEFT at Simmons

RIGHT on Milburn School Rd crossing IL 159 becoming E. O'Fallon Dr

Dairy Haven is at intersection of E. O'Fallon Dr. and IL Rte 157

RIGHT on IL 157 for 3 blocks

RIGHT at Hollywood Hts. and gear down for the 1/4 mile climb to top crossing IL 159 at stop light becomes Bethel Mine

Bear RIGHT at church Bethel Mine becomes Bethel School Rd (cycle east avoiding left turn on Witte Rd)

LEFT at O'Fallon-Troy Rd

Follow curve RIGHT on Seven Hills Rd

RIGHT at State St.

LEFT at railroad bridge

RIGHT on 1st

LEFT at Weber Dr and back to starting point, the Pedal-In.

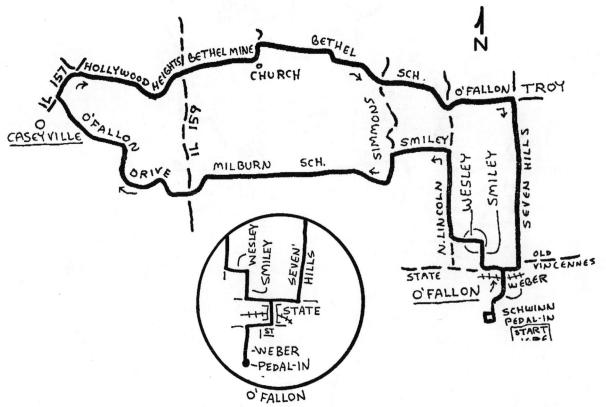

O'FALLON NORTHSIDE LOOP

Starting Point: Schwinn Pedal-In, East 50 Hwy, O'Fallon, IL
Distance: 26 miles
Approximate Pedaling Time: 2 hours
Terrain: Moderately rolling, lightly travelled country roads.
Things To See: A typical country ride east of the river.

This is a BABES ride given us by Ray Latimer. It starts in front of the Schwinn Pedal-In bike shop, East Hwy 50, O'Fallon, IL. Cycle north on Weber Rd.
RIGHT on 1st St.
LEFT across wooden railroad bridge. Exercise caution because bridge is narrow.
LEFT at State St.
RIGHT at 4-way stop on Smiley
LEFT on Wesley at school
RIGHT on North Lincoln
LEFT at Bethel School Rd - watch for on coming traffic
RIGHT at Witte and bear to right at Lemen Settlement
LEFT on Heck

LEFT on Lockmar
Continue straight on Lockmar Rd which begins a steep downhill after crossing Lebanon Rd;
then RIGHT with caution after passing under two railroad overpasses
RIGHT at W. Mill Creek Rd, a very nice, gently rolling country lane.
RIGHT at Blackjack Rd. tee which is Old Lebanon-Troy Rd and cycle for one mile

LEFT on Scott-Troy Rd.
RIGHT on Countyline Rd for a short climb

> *Shorter option:*
> Instead of turning on Countyline Rd, continue another 1/2 mile south on Scott-Troy with a RIGHT on Weil Rd.

RIGHT at Weil Rd. becoming Seven Hills Rd at intersection with O'Fallon-Troy Rd.
As the name implies, Seven Hills Rd has seven gently, rolling hills, mostly downhill into town.
RIGHT on State St
LEFT across the bridge
RIGHT on 1st
LEFT at Weber back to Pedal-In.

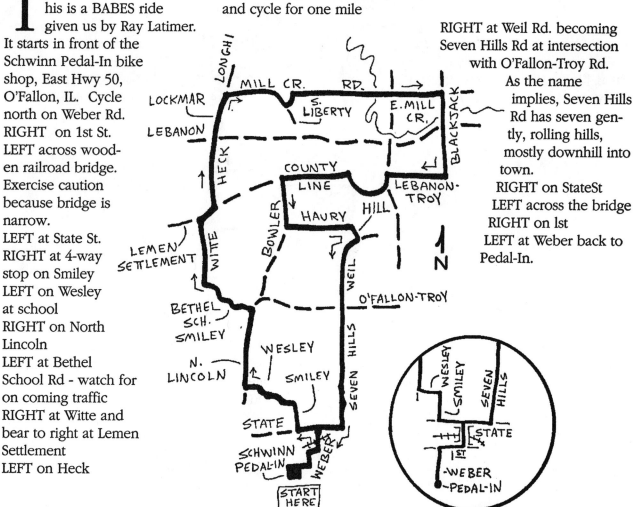
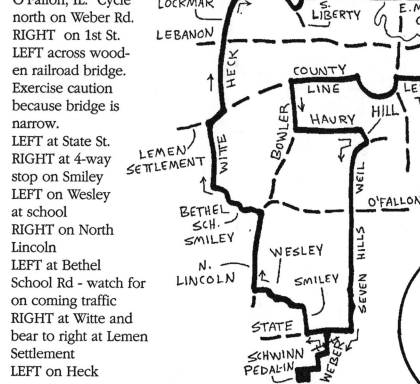

O'FALLON TO EDWARDSVILLE

Starting Point: Schwinn Pedal-In, East Hwy 50, O'Fallon
Distance: 41 miles
Approximate Pedaling Time: 2.5-3 hours
Terrain: Gently rolling
Things To See: Ray Latimer of the Belleview Area Bicycling and Eating Society(BABES) says "This is a really nice rural route with no hills to speak of and only one area of moderate traffic". The route can be ridden clockwise or counterclockwise but, because of congestion, counterclockwise is recommended.

Cycle from the front of Schwinn Pedal-In, across Hwy 50 and leave town on Weber St.
RIGHT at 1st St.
LEFT across railroad tracks on narrow, old wooden bridge.
RIGHT at State St. following curve left (avoid Old Vincennes)
LEFT(north) on Seven Hills Rd., these are seven gentle hills.
Cross O'Fallon—Troy Rd. which becomes Weill bending to right (eastbound)
LEFT on Scott-Troy Rd to stop sign
RIGHT at Old Lebanon-Troy Rd
LEFT at Blackjack
RIGHT 1/2 mile past E. Mill Creek on "unnamed road"
LEFT on Bauer Rd under railroad overpass
RIGHT at 40 Hwy just past flashing light
LEFT on Schlaeffer Rd.
LEFT on Schmalz
LEFT at Lower Marine Rd which feeds into Dewey
RIGHT at Clay St
RIGHT on Old Staunton Rd in Troy
LEFT on Maple Grove after crossing I-70
RIGHT on Old Staunton Rd (about 1/4 mile)

LEFT on Goshen Rd for 3.5 miles
LEFT at Village Dr into Edwardsville; for something to eat, there's plenty of fast food on Hwy 159 another 1/2 mile west.
LEFT on Old Troy Rd. passing under I-270
LEFT at Bouse Rd.
RIGHT at Frontage Rd
LEFT on IL 162 where it interesects with I-55; there's a major truck stop on the east side of I-55 so exercise care when crossing I-55
RIGHT at Formosa Rd. - if you arrive at fast food places, you've gone too far.
Follow IL 162 back to Formosa Rd - just before I-70 off ramp
Option: Bowler Rd shortens the route but it's narrow and curvy so be careful.
LEFT on W. Kirsch
RIGHT on N. Liberty
RIGHT at E. Mill Creek
LEFT at S. Liberty
RIGHT on Lebanon
LEFT on Bohnenstiel Rd
RIGHT at County Line
LEFT at Heck which become Witte
LEFT on Bethel School
RIGHT at stop sign on Troy-O'Fallon becoming N. Lincoln
LEFT at Wesley past school
RIGHT on Smiley
LEFT on State at 4-way
RIGHT across railroad bridge
RIGHT at 1st
LEFT at Weber to starting point

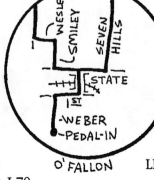

O'FALLON TO COLLINSVILLE

Starting Point: Schwinn Pedal-In, East Hwy 50, O'Fallon, IL.
Distance: 34 miles
Approximate Pedaling Time: 2.5-3 hours
Terrain: Mostly flat, several gentle grades, one or two hills
Things To See: A rural route over country roads compliments of Ray Latimer of the Belleville Area Bicycling and Eating Society (BABES)

From the front of the Pedal-In Bike Shop in O'Fallon, IL on E. Hwy 50.
Cycle north on Weber
RIGHT at 1st
LEFT across railroad bridge
LEFT at State
RIGHT at
Smiley 4-way
LEFT on Wesley at school
RIGHT on N. Lincoln
LEFT at Smiley Rd
LEFT at Simmons
RIGHT on Milburn School Rd (use caution in crossing IL Hwy 159)
Continue on East O'Fallon Drive
LEFT on Pleasant Ridge
RIGHT at Bunkum
RIGHT at Circle Dr with caution descending hill
LEFT (east) on O'Fallon

RIGHT on Center
RIGHT on Hollywood Heights cross IL 159 at stoplight; becomes Bethel Mine Rd
LEFT at stop sign, church on right
RIGHT at S. Clinton which becomes Bethel Meadows
RIGHT on Black Jack
RIGHT on Lebanon
RIGHT at Mulberry Rd
LEFT at Lemen Settlement
LEFT on Heck
RIGHT on Lebanon Rd
RIGHT at Bohnenstiel Rd
LEFT at Haury Rd, short, steep climb just before Weil
RIGHT on Weil crossing O'Fallon-Troy and becomes Seven Hills Rd
RIGHT at State St
LEFT across railroad bridge
RIGHT at 1st
LEFT on Weber to starting point

O'FALLON TO SMITHTON

Starting Point: Schwinn Pedal-In, East Hwy 50, O'Fallon, IL.
Distance: 55 miles
Approximate Pedaling Time: 4 hours
Terrain: Mostly flat with two or three long, gentle grades
Things To See: Ray Latimer of BABES says Erma's Restaurant in Smithton really makes this ride worthwhile.

Cycle from Schwinn Pedal-In west on E. Hwy 50 for 3 blocks
LEFT on Southview
RIGHT at Westminister
Left on S. Lincoln becomes Shiloh.
O'Fallon Rd becomes Cross St.
RIGHT at Main at stop sign
LEFT at Shiloh Station at Stagecoach (a landmark in Shiloh)
LEFT at Hwy 161
RIGHT on Radio Range Rd (marked by radio antennae)
LEFT on IL 158
RIGHT at Rentchler Rd
LEFT at T intersection which becomes Renneck Rd
LEFT on Jefferson Rd at intersection with Jacks Run Rd
RIGHT on Engelmann Township

RIGHT at Pleasant Ridge Rd
RIGHT at Long Lake Rd across IL 15 south becomes Suemmicht Rd then E Road
RIGHT on 5 Forks Rd crossing IL 13

RIGHT on Robinson School Rd
LEFT at Blacksmith
LEFT at Yeager (gravel pile)
RIGHT on Brenner
LEFT on Press into Smithton and Erma's Restaurant
Leave on Press Rd
LEFT at Kraft which becomes Holcomb School Rd and then Hill 9 Rd
LEFT after railroad tracks on unnamed road into Freeburg
RIGHT on Apple St
LEFT on Vine
RIGHT at Mill
LEFT at Jacks Run Rd intersection of IL 15 a convenience store
Continue on Jacks Run Rd and at White Oaks Club Rd GO NORTH, the sign is turned the wrong way.
LEFT 1/2 mile parallel than cross railroad tracks
RIGHT on Jefferson
LEFT on Rentschler
LEFT at Dunlap which becomes Plum Hill School Rd (use caution descending with sharp left)
RIGHT at IL 158
LEFT on Radio Range
LEFT on IL 161
RIGHT at Shiloh Station
RIGHT at Stagecoach
LEFT at stop sign
RIGHT on Westminister
LEFT on Southview
RIGHT at E 50 Hwy to Pedal-In

O'FALLON TO FREEBURG LOOP

Starting Point: Schwin Pedal-In, E. Hwy 50, O'Fallon, IL
Distance: 56 miles
Approximate Pedaling Time: 4.5-5 hours
Terrain: Gently rolling hills
Things To See: This BABES rides is north-south and can be challenging if windy. There's food in Freeburg at Gary's Restaurant or Tom's Foodland.

Cross Hwy 50 to Weber
LEFT on Third St
LEFT on S. Lincoln
RIGHT at Main St. in Shiloh
LEFT at Shiloh Station Rd
LEFT on IL Rt 161
RIGHT on Radio Range Rd
LEFT at IL Rt 177
RIGHT at Rentschler Sta. Rd
LEFT on Rentschler Mine Rd
RIGHT on Funk School Rd
RIGHT at Jefferson Rd
LEFT at Funk School Rd
LEFT on Jacks Run Rd
Stay to right on Jefferson Rd
RIGHT at Brickyard (Englleman Twp)
RIGHT at Pleasant School Rd
RIGHT on Karch Rd
Cross Rt. 15 to Mueller
Straight on Five Forks Rd
Cross Rt 13 to Robinson School
LEFT before rock pile
RIGHT on Brenner Rd
Cross Press Rd to Kraft Rd
Straight on Holcomb School Rd (Karft turns left)
LEFT on IL Rt 13 to Freeburg
RIGHT at Apple St (stop light)
LEFT at Pitts
RIGHT on Cemetery

LEFT on Barber
LEFT at Jacks Run Rd
RIGHT at White Oaks Club Rd
RIGHT on Jefferson Rd
LEFT on Rentschler Rd
LEFT at Plum Hill Rd (Dunlap)
LEFT at IL Rt 177
RIGHT on Green Mount Rd
Cross 161 onto Little Oak Ln
LEFT at Shiloh Rd (no sign)

RIGHT at St. Clair Twp Line Rd
Cross US Rt 50
RIGHT on W.State St
Caution!!! Bad railroad track
RIGHT on N. Lincoln
LEFT at E. Third St
RIGHT at Weber St.
Finish at Pedal-In

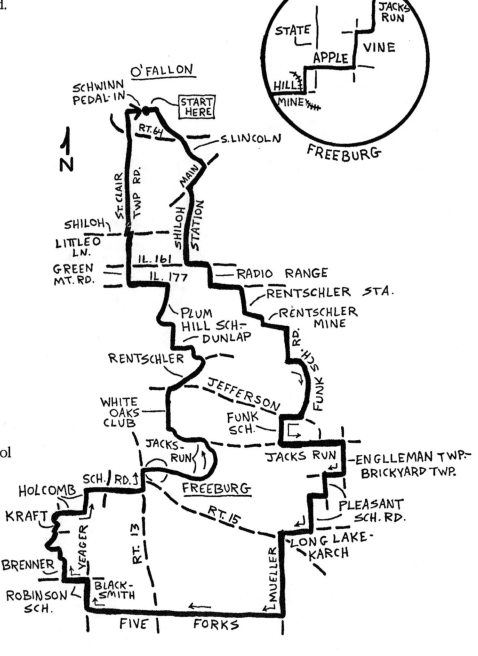

FAIRVIEW HEIGHTS-COLLINSVILLE LOOP

Starting Point: The Touring Cyclist, Old US 50 & Hwy 159
Distance: 33 miles
Approximate Pedaling Time: 2.5-3 hours
Terrain: Mostly flat, with some rolling hills
Things To See: John Werner says this ride offers nice country riding plus some city "stuff". Lunch at Becker's Restaurant in Collinsville.

LEFT at Keebler
RIGHT on Harding
RIGHT on Rebecca for lunch at Becker's Restaurant (16.5 miles)
RIGHT at Vandalia
LEFT at Spring
LEFT on Lebanon Rd and stay to left at intersection
RIGHT on Clay School Rd
RIGHT at Longhi Rd

RIGHT at Lockmann Rd
Stay LEFT at Tee intersection on Lebanon Rd
RIGHT on Heck Rd
RIGHT on Witte Rd
RIGHT at Bethel School Rd
LEFT at Simmons Rd
RIGHT on Milburn School Rd
LEFT on Old Collinsville Rd
RIGHT at Drake
RIGHT to starting point

Cycle south from Touring Cyclist store
LEFT at Drake
LEFT at Old Collinsville Rd across Old Hwy 50
LEFT on Millburn School across Hwy 159
Continue into E. O'Fallon Dr
RIGHT on Hwy 157 at Caseyville
RIGHT on Hollywood Hts.Rd with big uphill becomes Bethel Mine Rd when crossing Hwy 159
LEFT at church
LEFT at S.Clinton Rd across Hwy 159 again
RIGHT on Cemetery
LEFT on Center
RIGHT at Juda

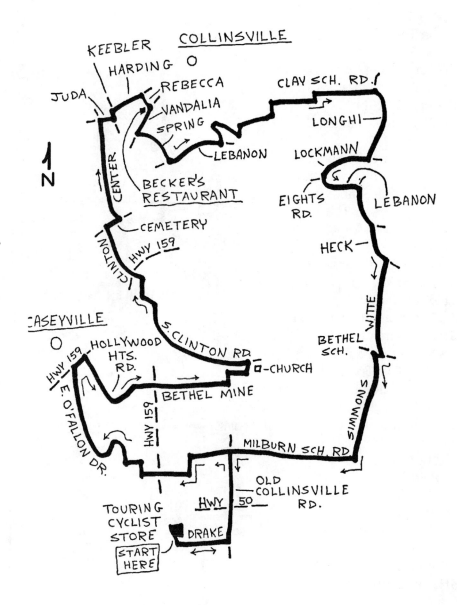

FAIRVIEW HEIGHTS LOOP

Starting Point: Fairview Hts, Hwy 159 & Drake
Distance: 24 miles
Approximate Pedaling Time: 2 hours
Terrain: Mostly flat with a few rolling hills
Things To See: This is a 24 mile loop on country roads that passes Belleville, O'Fallon, and Fairview Heights.

Cycle east on Drake
RIGHT on Old Collinsville Rd
LEFT on Thovenot
RIGHT at Hartmann Ln
LEFT at stoplight
RIGHT on Anderson Ln
LEFT on East B St. Rd which becomes Shiloh Station West
LEFT at Shiloh Station

RIGHT at Shiloh Rd past a 4-way stop and then a stoplight
LEFT on Rieder at fork past stop at Hwy 50
LEFT on Silver Creek Rd then first right
LEFT at Hagemann Rd which, at 4-way stop, becomes O'Fallon-Troy Rd
LEFT (west) on Bethel School Rd
LEFT on Simmons which then becomes Porter Rd
RIGHT at Frontage Rd
LEFT at Old Collinsville Rd
RIGHT on Drake to starting point.

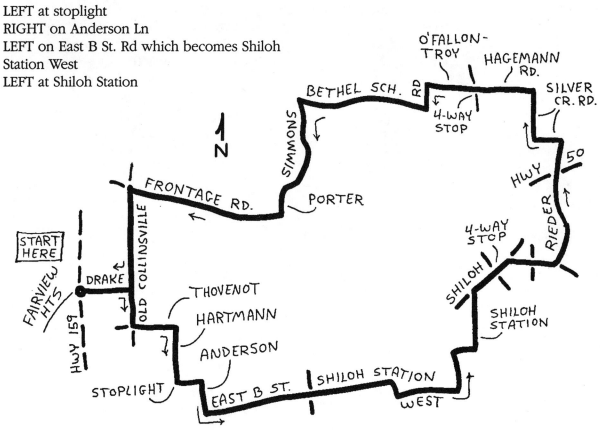

HIGHLAND–PICKNEYVILLE TOUR

Starting Point: Highland, IL Senior High, on I-70 east from St. Louis
Distance: 153 miles over 2 days
Approximate Pedaling Time: 2 days
Terrain: Mostly flat
Things To See: This 2-lane ride on blacktop through Illinois countryside can be divided into several one day loops.

RIGHT from Highland High School parking lot.
RIGHT at stop sign on Rt 160
LEFT at junction Rt 143/40 and Rt 160
Straight on Rt 143/40
RIGHT on Rt 143 to Pierron
CONTINUE through Pierron
RIGHT at Barnhardt St to Jamestown and Breese (water & rest rooms)
RIGHT at stop sign - Junction Rt 50
LEFT on Germantown Rd (Shell Station on corner) into Germantown
RIGHT at stop sign onto Rt 161 into Albers
LEFT at Damiansville Rd and straight past Damiansville
Cross I-64
Straight at stop sign at Clinton Co. Rd 300E
LEFT at stop sign onto Rt 160
LEFT at stop sign Junction Rts 160 & 177 - stay on Rt 160
Enter Okawville (48 miles)
RIGHT at stop sign, stay on Rt 160
Bear left at Y intersection into Addieville
LEFT at stop sign Junction with

Rt 15 - towards Nashville
Enter Nashville(60.6 miles)
RIGHT onto Rt 127 (south)
Enter Pickneyville (80 miles)
RIGHT aon Rt 13 (west) at town square
LEFT onto Rt 154 at Y intersection
Enter Eden - go right on Rt 153 (north)
Enter Coulterville (103 miles)
LEFT at stop sign onto Rt 153/13
RIGHT, follow Rt 153 (North)
RIGHT at junction with Rt 15 (east)
LEFT on Okawville Rd
Enter

Okawville (123.7 miles)
LEFT at junction with Rt 160 and stay on Rt 160
RIGHT at junction Rts 160 & 177 - stay on Rt 160 (north)
CROSS I-64
Junction 160 & 161, stay on Rt 161 (north) water at liquor store
Continue on 160 at stop sign
Enter Madison County (145 miles)
Enter Highland
RIGHT at stop sign, stay on 160
LEFT on Poplar - traffic signal
Bear left on Poplar - do not follow 160
Straight at stop sign - Junction 40
LEFT at Troxler Rd
LEFT into High School parking lot (152.8 miles)

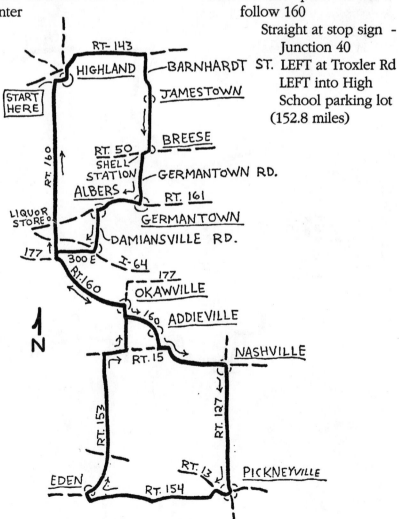

BAC WEDNESDAY NITE RIDE

Starting Point: Belleville Area College, Belleville, IL
Distance: 12 miles
Approximate Pedaling Time: 1.5 hours
Terrain: Rolling hills
Things To See: This is a BABES Wedneday night ride furnished by David Weidler. Sights include Knobloch Woods Nature Area; Westerfield House B & B; Eckert's Orchard Store for ice cream.

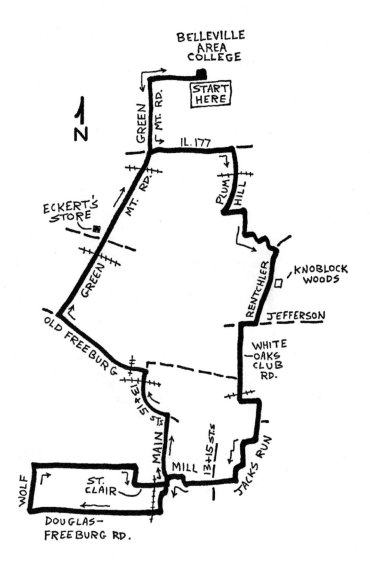

Cycle south from BAC on Green Mtn Rd
LEFT on IL 177
RIGHT on Plum Hill Rd and up a hill
RIGHT at Rentschler Rd past Knobloch Woods Nature area
RIGHT at Jefferson Rd
LEFT on White Oaks Club Rd and across railroad tracks
LEFT and then right on Jack's Run Rd across 13 & 15 Sts
Continue on Mill St
LEFT at Main St for loop
RIGHT on Douglas-Freeburg Rd across railroad tracks
RIGHT at Wolf Rd
RIGHT at St. Clair across railroad tracks
LEFT on Main St
LEFT on 13 & 15 Sts at intersection across more tracks
LEFT at Old Freeburg Rd
RIGHT at Green Mtn. Rd with a stop at Eckert's Orchard store for ice cream
Continue north on Green Mtn. Rd back to the starting point

EVER SEE A SINK HOLE?

Starting Point: Millstadt City Park, Jefferson Barracks Bridge via Rt 3, east on Hwy 158
Distance: 19 miles
Approximate Pedaling Time: 1.5-2 hours
Terrain: Mostly flat
Things To See: This ride is a favorite of Tom Yarbrough(SLBTS). Spectacular views of "sink holes" and of downtown St. Louis in April and May. Eckert's apple orchard in September and beautiful colors in October. Places to eat and drink in Millstadt.

Cycle from Millstadt City Park south on Main St.
RIGHT on Washington
RIGHT on Kropp
LEFT at Bluffside
RIGHT at Stemler
RIGHT on Old Columbia which becomes Wagner
RIGHT on Otten
LEFT at Forest Hill
RIGHT at Mueller
RIGHT on Zingg
LEFT on Saeger which becomes Polk
LEFT at Parkview
RIGHT at Main St. into Millstadt

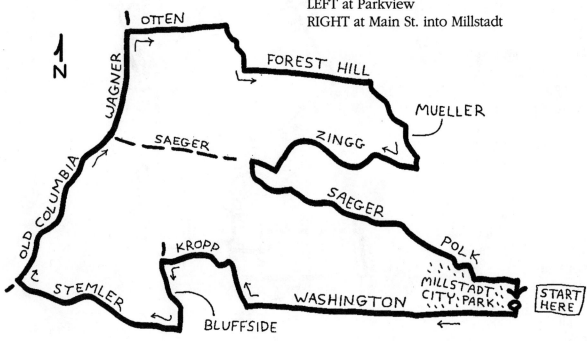

COLUMBIA TO WATERLOO

Starting Point: Columbia, IL Market Place behind McDonald's
Distance: 35 Miles and 54 Miles
Approximate Pedaling Time: 3 Hours and 4 Hours
Terrain: Moderately hilly
Things To See: Very scenic ride; Lincoln Trail Restaurant in Waterloo is good.

Cycle north from Market Place
RIGHT on Sand Bank, a steep hill, and across Rt 3 becoming Main St
LEFT on Cherry St for another hill and becomes Bluffside
RIGHT at Stemmler becoming Bohleyville when crossing Hwy 158
LEFT at Lake Gilmore Rd
RIGHT on Bohleyville Rd curving left into Hammacher and Waterloo
LEFT on Rt 3 to Rogers St and the Lincoln Trail Restaurant
Exit Waterloo north on Rt 3
LEFT at Columbia
RIGHT at Moore
LEFT on HH Rd
RIGHT on Gall Rd
LEFT at Hanover Rd
RIGHT at D Rd with interesting church on left
LEFT on Bluff Rd at Old Valmeyer

54 Mile OPTION

Cycle north from Market Place
RIGHT at Sand Bank, up hill, and across Rt 3 becoming Main St.
LEFT at Cherry which becomes Old Columbia Rd and then Wagner Rd
RIGHT on Hertel School Rd
RIGHT on Saeger
LEFT at Triple Lakes Rd P53 when crossing Hwy 158 becomes Bohleyville Rd
RIGHT at Floraville Rd P57 which becomes Hammacher Rd into Waterloo
LEFT on Rt 3 to Rogers St and the Lincon Trail Restaurant.
Return to Columbia the same way.

COLUMBIA TO FREEBURG TOUR

Starting Point: Columbia Grade School, south on IL Rt 3, Columbia, IL
Distance: 55 miles
Approximate Pedaling Time: 4-5 hours
Terrain: Flat to rolling hills
Things To See: This out and back ride is another favorite of Jim Jeske. All travel is on two lane blacktop. There's food/drink in Millstadt, Smithton, and Freeburg.

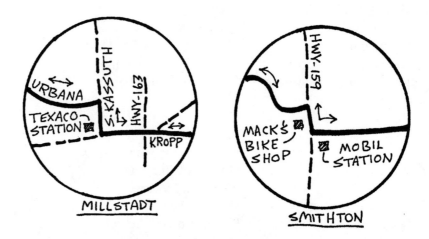

Cycle from Columbia Grade School east on Main St
LEFT on Cherry
RIGHT on Old Columbia Rd
RIGHT at Bluffside Rd
LEFT at Kropp Rd with red brick house on right into Millstadt
Cross Hwy 163
RIGHT on S. Kassuth, the street before the Texaco Station
LEFT on Urbana Rd and follow with a series of right and left turns north into Smithton
RIGHT on Hwy 159 with Mobil Station on left
LEFT at Mack's Bike Shop
Continue into Freeburg
LEFT at Hwy 13 to Davis Cup Drive-In
Return to Columbia the same route

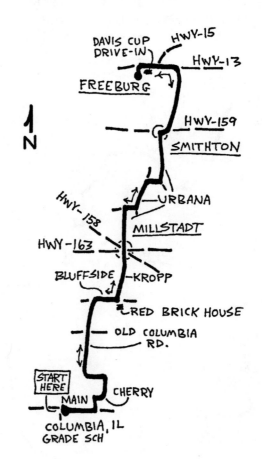

WATERLOO TO PRAIRIE DU ROCHER

Starting Point: Hwy 156
(Maeystown Rd), Waterloo, IL
Distance: 87 miles
Approximate Pedaling Time:
5-6 hours
Terrain: Rolling hills
Things To See: Prairie du
Rocher is a nice old French
town. Lunch at Lisa's.

Cycle south from
Waterloo on Hwy 156
(Maeystown Rd)
LEFT on KK
RIGHT at Bushy Prairie to
Maeystown
LEFT at Franklin (LL)
RIGHT on Kaskaskia
LEFT on VV
RIGHT at Ames
LEFT at Hwy 155 to Ruma
RIGHT on 1st St before Hwy 3
past power transformer
RIGHT on Modoc Rd
RIGHT at Bluff Rd into Prairie
du Rocher (Lunch at Lisa's)

Return to Waterloo the same
route

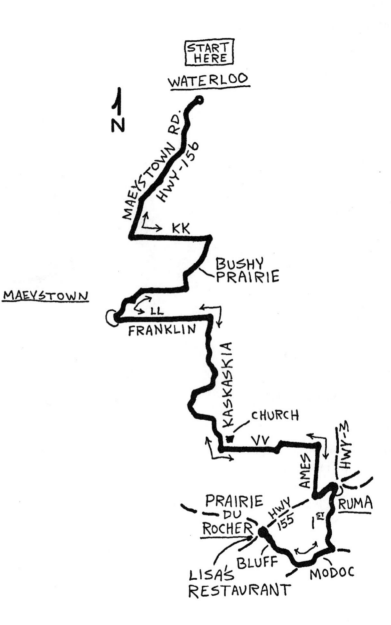

75

WATERLOO TO MAEYSTOWN LOOP

Starting Point: Gibault High School, Rt 3 south from I-255, Waterloo, IL
Distance: 60 miles
Approximate Pedaling Time: 4.5-5.5 hours
Terrain: Flat to rolling hills
Things To See: This is a favorite ride of Jim Jeske. It's typical southern Illinois terrain. Food and drink can be found in Wartburg, Renault, Prairie du Rocher, and Maeystown.

Cycle on Country Club Lane across Hwy 3
LEFT at first intersection on Monroe (toward Waterloo)
RIGHT on to Hwy 156 (Park St) across railroad tracks
LEFT at Lakeview Dr (toward Wartburg/Maeystown) and pass through Wartburg
LEFT at second turn (K.K. Rd) with microwave tower on right
RIGHT on new paved road in Burksville
Cycle through St. Joe, Renault, and pass Lake Mildred signs - down major hill
LEFT on Bluff Rd for food/drink in Prairie du Rocher
Continue past Fort Chartres and Kidd
RIGHT before levee to Fults
LEFT at Bluff Rd
RIGHT into Maeystown for food/drink
Return through Maeystown, up a hill, and follow main road back to Waterloo

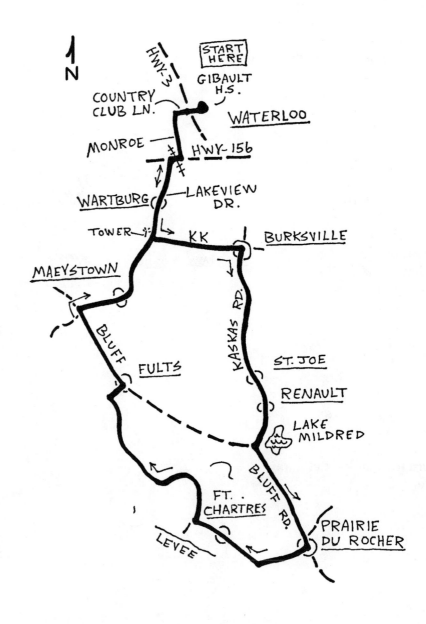

NEW BADEN TO HIGHLAND

Starting Point: City Park, New Baden, IL.
Distance: Short route 42 miles; Long route about 60 miles
Approximate Pedaling Time: 3.5 hours & 5 hours
Terrain: Mostly flat
Things To See: Ray Latimer of BABES says, "this is an honest-to-goodness flat ride". St. Jacob is home of the Strawberry Festival in May. The House of Plenty in Highland is a good place to eat. A scenic country ride.

Cycle from New Baden's City Park west on Illinois through New Baden
RIGHT at County Line
LEFT at Pfeiffer
RIGHT on Summerfield Rd where there's a convenience store
LEFT on Lilac
RIGHT on Summerfield into St. Jacob
RIGHT at old Shell Station on Ellis Rd
LEFT at Old Trenton Rd to Highland and the Horn of Plenty on 9th St
RIGHT on 13th
LEFT on Mulberry
RIGHT at 9th for food
RIGHT at Laurel St
LEFT on 13th

RIGHT at Washington
LEFT on Lindenthal Ave
RIGHT on Poplar
LEFT at Arkansas Rd
LEFT on Buckeye
RIGHT at Arkansas, and head south with jogs
LEFT at first chance county road 130E,until intersecting IL 160 just north of Trenton (or,RIGHT at Neiss Rd (32 miles) and LEFT IL Hwy 160 easier)

The short route continues south on IL 160
RIGHT at Grove School Rd
LEFT on County Rd
LEFT on Illinois thru New

The long route makes 1st left on Mill St after the railroad tracks heading east for Germantown
LEFT at Rockyford Rd
RIGHT on Highline at T inter-section
RIGHT on Grassy Branch
LEFT at Wesclin Rd
RIGHT at Drive-In Rd
RIGHT on Patricia
LEFT on Woodlawn
RIGHT at Monterrey
LEFT at Hunter
RIGHT on Nunsey into Damiansville
RIGHT on Billhartz
LEFT at Hazelhorst
RIGHT at IL 160
RIGHT into Park

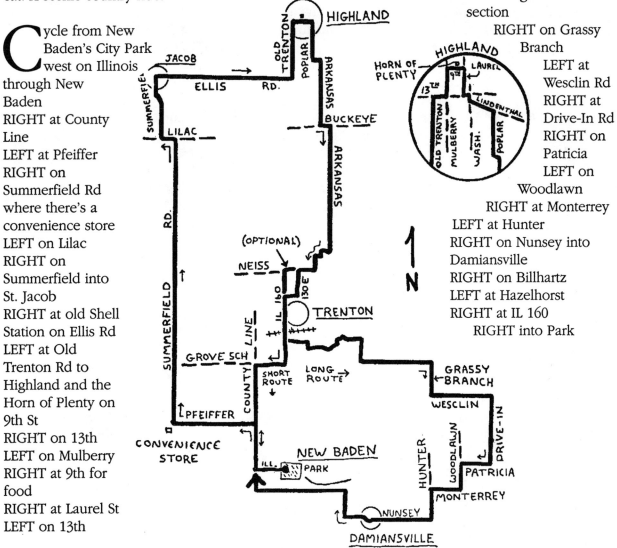

77

NATALIE KEKEISEN MEMORIAL "FLAT AS A PANCAKE" CENTURY©

Starting Point: New Baden, IL on S. Hwy 160. Take I-64 east from St. Louis
Distance: 100 miles
Approximate Pedaling Time: ????
Terrain: "Flat as a pancake"
Things To See: Since this guide is about "day rides", we have avoided century rides and over-nighters. But, a cyclist who rides at least twice a week, or more than 50 miles a week, can certainly do a flat century towards the end of the cycling season. This is an OAC/AYH annual ride in memory of Natalie G. Kekeisan, a most important figure in St. Louis cycling. It can be ridden as a 66 miler.

RIGHT on S. Hwy 160 from New Baden Park
LEFT on Hwy 177/160
RIGHT at Venedy Station Rd
RIGHT at Pecan St
LEFT on Mill St
RIGHT on Church St
LEFT at 300E (Kinyon Rd)
Straight across IL 15
LEFT on 900N (unmarked) at Johannesburg School
Straight across Hwy 153
LEFT on 800E at Tee (unmarked)
RIGHT at IL Hwy 15
RIGHT at 1030E/Red Plum Hill Church Rd (unmarked)(25.5 miles)
LEFT on 800N at Tee (South Grand)

Straight at stop sign across Co. Hwy 21 (no marker)
Cross rough railroad tracks
Straight around curve past hospital
LEFT on W. Alton St. - Nashsville
LEFT on S. Prairie St.
RIGHT at Belleville St
RIGHT at Bryant St (Friendship Manor Nursing Home)(35 miles)
RIGHT on W. Lebanon St
LEFT on S. Grand St.
Cross W. St. Louis St (Hwy 15)
Cross 6 sets of rough tracks
Bear left and cross culvert
RIGHT at 1600E (unmarked)
Straight at junction
Cross railroad tracks
Cross County Hwy 4
LEFT on Main St
Cross IL 160 and continue on Hwy 6 to Addieville Park(44 miles)
RIGHT on 800E (Okawville Rd)(unmarked)(3 silos to right)
LEFT on 1350N (White Church Rd)
RIGHT at 500E at Tee (unmarked)
LEFT at IL 160/177 - rough railroad tracks
LEFT on 170E
RIGHT on 000E (County Line Rd)
Cross Hwy 177
Cross over I-64
RIGHT on Illinois St.
RIGHT into New Baden Park (66 miles)

More than a metric century and an option to go home

LEFT on Illinois St
RIGHT on Clinton
RIGHT at 1100N
Cross IL 160
LEFT at 180E
RIGHT on 1150N
LEFT on 350E
LEFT at Tee (unmarked)
LEFT at 520E
RIGHT on 4th St (Aviston)
Jog straight on 4th
LEFT at 600E
RIGHT at 1380N
RIGHT on 900E
LEFT on 1400N
RIGHT at 950E (N. Walnut St) and enter Breese
Jog south at stop sign
LEFT at Tee (JLF Apts)
RIGHT immediately on S. Walnut
Cross over pancake "lump"
RIGHT on 1100N
LEFT on 800E
RIGHT at 1000N
LEFT at 700E
Cross IL 161 (caution)
RIGHT on 700N
LEFT on 600E
RIGHT at 600N, straight through Damiansville
RIGHT at 300N
LEFT on 700N
RIGHT on 100E (IL 160)
LEFT into New Baden Park

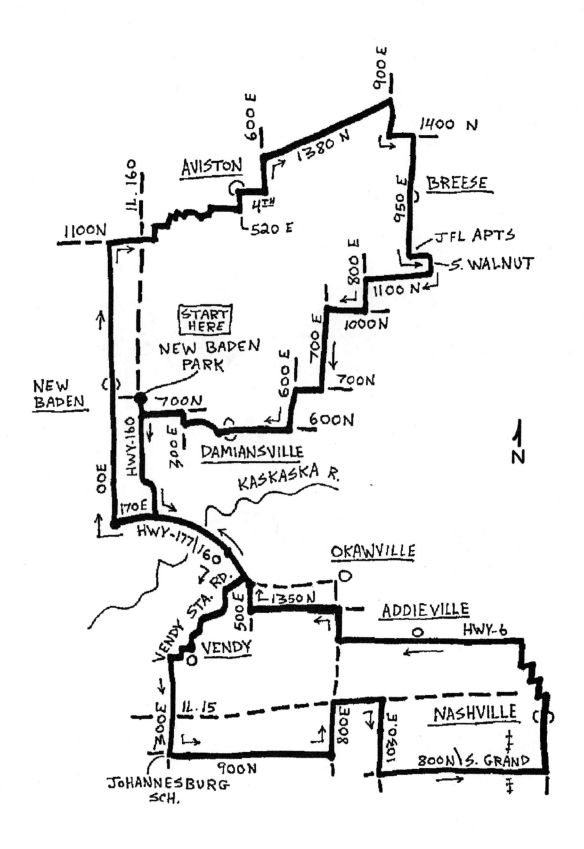

MASCOUTAH TO WILLISVILLE

Starting Point: Scheve Park, Mascoutah, IL, Water Tower & Red Caboose
Distance: 47 miles each way
Approximate Pedaling Time: 6.5 hours
Terrain: Mostly flat with occasional rolling hills
Things To See: Wind is a factor in cycling the metro east sector while the hills are generally not. A wind from the north or south can make this ride challenging says Ray Latimer of BABES. The Pioneer Cabin Restaurant in Willisville is your reward.

LEFT at Johannesburg School thru remains of Stone Church, IL. RIGHT on IL Rt 153 south to Lively Grove and on to Coulterville; stop at Dairy Queen or Casey's General Store
LEFT on IL 13
RIGHT just past Perry County

line sign to Willisville; traffic is light but fast so ride single file. Crossing IL 150 road becomes Rt 4 into Willisville; watch for signs to Pioneer Cabin Restaurant about 1/2 east of town.
Return to Mascoutah the same route.

Cycle on from Scheve Park in Mascoutah, IL, clearly marked by a water tower and red caboose.
RIGHT on IL Rt 4
LEFT on IL Rt 177, the only way across Kaskasia River
RIGHT at grain elevator thru Venedy past church with steeple, south out of town and across IL Rt 15

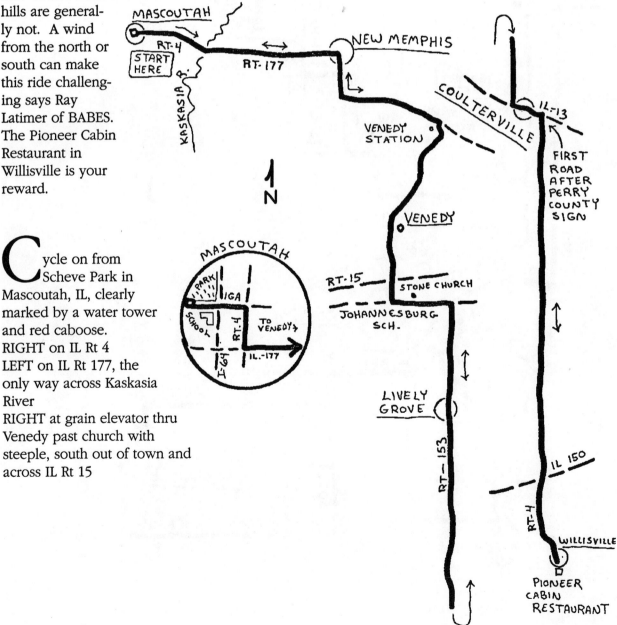

MASCOUTAH TO NEW ATHENS

Starting Point: Scheve Park, Mascoutah, IL, Hwy 177 south of Scott AFB
Distance: 50 miles
Approximate Pedaling Time: 4 hours
Terrain: Mostly flat
Things To See: Peacock Site Tavern in New Athens is "bicycle friendly" says Dave Weidler of BABES

Cycle from Scheve Park east
RIGHT on Jefferson (Rt 4)
LEFT on Rt 15
RIGHT at Bee Hollow Rd
RIGHT at Lichenbrock School Rd
RIGHT on Pleasant Ridge Rd
LEFT on Eckert Rd
RIGHT at Darmstadt Rd

LEFT at Lenzberg Rd
RIGHT on Schaller Rd
RIGHT on Baldwin Rd
LEFT at Dutch Hill School Rd
RIGHT at Keim Rd (no sign)
LEFT on Peacock Site Rd (look for white arrow) to Tavern
LEFT on Rt 13
RIGHT at Werner Rd
RIGHT at Old Sand Rd
LEFT on Black Quarter Rd

RIGHT on Five Forks Rd
LEFT at Lone Star Rd (Short route, 30 miles, continues straight as follows
RIGHT at Rt 15
LEFT on Pleasant Ridge School Rd
LEFT on Drum Hill Rd
LEFT at Brickyard Rd
RIGHT on Harnett to Scheve Park
Longer route continues east on Five Forks Rd for another loop past Tavern

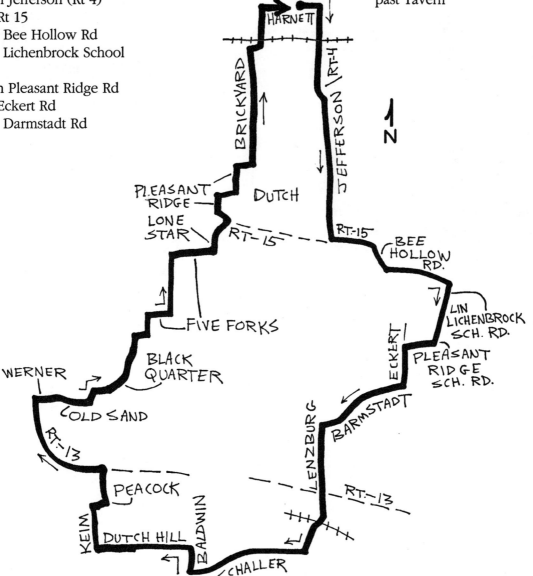

81

MASCOUTAH THREE COUNTRY RIDE

Starting Point: Scheve Park, Mascoutah, IL
Distance: 27 miles
Approximate Pedaling Time: 2 hours
Terrain: Mostly flat
Things To See: Dave Weidler of BABES suggests lunch at Eagle's Nest in Addieville, and a stop to see the mineral baths on Okawville, on this 3 county ride.

Cycle from Scheve Park
RIGHT on Fuesser Rd
RIGHT on Woodland School Rd
LEFT at IL Rt 177
RIGHT at Liebig School Rd
LEFT on Zimmermann Rd
RIGHT on Clinton Co. Line Rd
LEFT at Bottom Rd
RIGHT at State Rt 177
RIGHT on County Hwy 12
LEFT on Locust St (Venedy)
RIGHT at Front St
Lunch at Eagle's Nest in Addieville

LEFT on N. Center St
LEFT on Cardinal Rd (road curves right; turn left)
LEFT at Cardinal Rd
RIGHT at Hummingbird Rd
RIGHT on Hen House Rd   to Dairy Queen
RIGHT on Hanover St in Okawville
LEFT at Fourth St (to bypass town)
LEFT at High St (Rt 177)
RIGHT on Rt 177
RIGHT on 4th St in New Memphis
LEFT at Center St
RIGHT at State Rt 160
LEFT on Airport Rd
RIGHT on IL Rt 177
RIGHT at 6th St

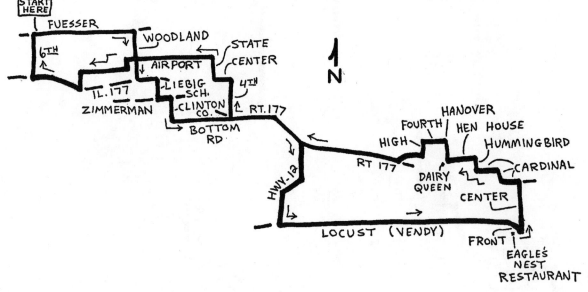

HOUSE OF PLENTY RIDE

Starting Point: Scheve Park in Mascoutah, IL
Distance: 50 miles
Approximate Pedaling Time: 3.5-4 hours
Terrain: Flat
Things To See: Dave Weidler of BABES recommends the House of Plenty in Highland for lunch, thus the name of the ride. Also, about 2 miles south of Highland after lunch is the Latzer Homestead, the "inventor of Pet Milk".

Cycle east from Scheve Park
LEFT on 6th
RIGHT on Faust
LEFT at Korte-Sewald (no sign)
RIGHT at Oak Grove School Rd
LEFT on Summerfield So. Rd over tracks and past City Park
RIGHT on Pleasant Valley School Rd
LEFT at Old Trenton
RIGHT at Rutz Rd
LEFT on Sportmen
LEFT on Buckeye

RIGHT at Arkansas Rd
LEFT at Lindenthal Ave
RIGHT at Washington
LEFT on 9th for lunch at the House of Plenty
LEFT on Walnut
RIGHT at 13th
LEFT at Chestnut
RIGHT on Ellis
LEFT on Chestnut
RIGHT at Lilac
LEFT at Summerfield
RIGHT joining IL 161
LEFT at 6th
RIGHT on Harnett to Scheve Park

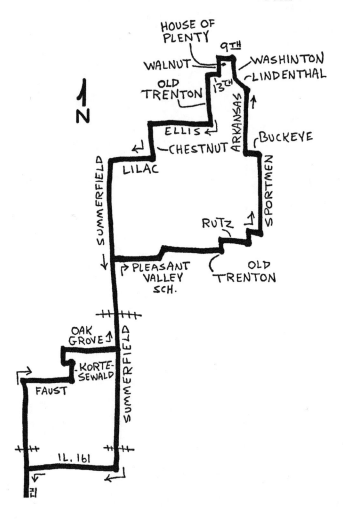

TOUR DE CURE©

Starting Point: Raging Rivers Water Park, Grafton, IL
Distance: 25, 50, and 100 miles
Approximate Pedaling Time: Day long celebration
Terrain: Flat
Things To See: The Tour de Cure is an annual cycling event held throughout the country for the benefit of the American Diabetes Association. It's for novice, intermediate, and veteran cyclists. There's a participants' party at the water park following the ride. Most important, it helps the many people with diabetes. This ride is scheduled for June 26 in 1994

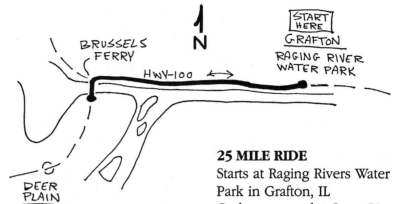

25 MILE RIDE

Starts at Raging Rivers Water Park in Grafton, IL
Cycle west on the Great River Rd
Ride the Brussels free ferry over and back
Return the same route to the water park.

50 MILE RIDE

Starts at Raging Rivers Water Park in Grafton, IL
Cycle west on the Great River Rd
Continue north on Rt 100 along Pere Marquette State Park
Becomes Rt 16 at Nutwood (Rt 100/16)
Free ferry across Illinois River to Hardin
South at Hardin on Rt 100
Stay left at Brussels throough Deer Plain to Brussels free ferry
RIGHT on Rt 100 (Great River Rd)after ferry ride to water park

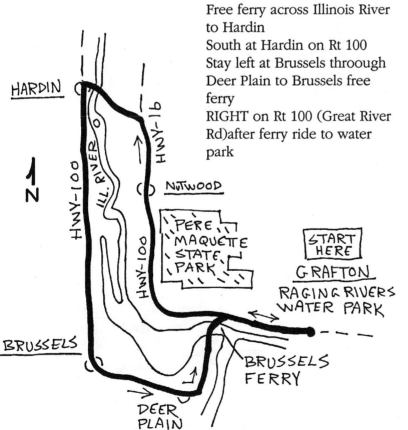

TOUR DE CURE©

100 MILE RIDE
Starts at Raging Rivers Water
Park in Grafton, IL
Cycle west on the Great River
Rd
Continue north on Rt 100
along Pere Marquette State
Park
Becomes Rt 16 at Nutwood (Rt
100/16)
Becomes Eldred Rd at Spankey
RIGHT on Woody Rd
LEFT on Hwy 267
LEFT at Carrollton
Continue west on Rt 108 at
Eldred for the free ferry
Continue through Kampsville
on Rt 96

LEFT on Rt 96
LEFT at Hamburg Rd
RIGHT at Rt 100 south past
Hardin and Brussels
Stay left at Brussels through
Deer Plain to Brussels free
ferry
RIGHT on Rt 100 after ferry
ride to water park

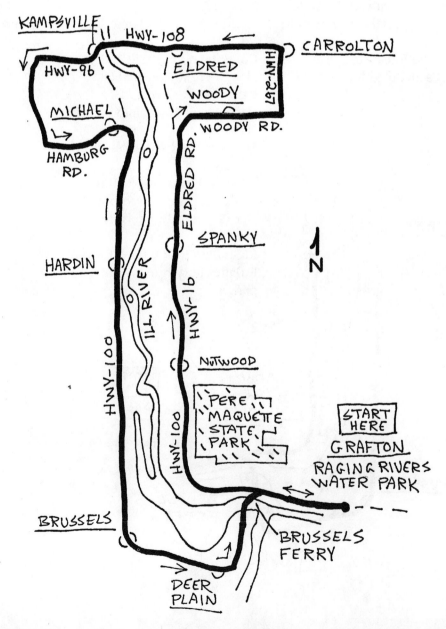

ILLLINOIS RIVER RIDE

Starting Point: Pere Marquette State Park Lodge, from Alton, IL via River Road
Distance: 84 miles
Approximate Pedaling Time: 6-7 hours
Terrain: Flat to rolling hills on 2 lane blacktop
Things To See: A favorite ride of Jim Jeske. Excellent food at Pere Marquestte Lodge with taverns at Nutwood & Hillview and snacks at White Hall, Belltown, & Eldred

Cycle north from Pere Marquette Park on Hwy 100
CONTINUE on 16/100 after Nutwood; becomes Eldred Rd after Spankey
CONTINUE north at Eldred
RIGHT at Hillview
RIGHT at White Hall on Hwy 267
RIGHT at Carrollton on Hwy 108
LEFT at Eldred and follow Eldred Rd south
CONTINUE south at Spankey on Hwy 16/100 to Pere Marquette State Park.

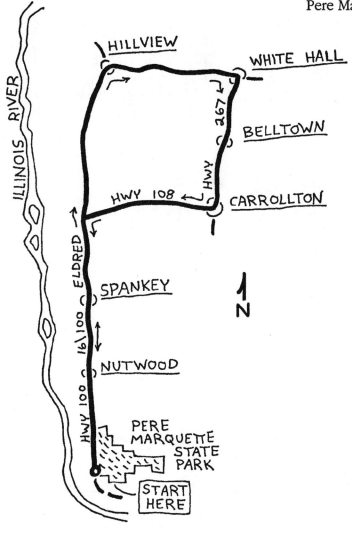

TOUR OF SAM BAKER STATE PARK

Starting Point: Sam Baker State Park, I-55 south, Mo Hwy 67 south, west on Hwy34
Distance: 65 miles first day, 55 miles second day.
Approximate Pedaling Time: ????
Terrain: Hilly
Things To See: It's a long time "between drinks" so bring snacks. Great food at Zephyr Cafe on first day's ride says Jim Jeske. On second day there's a couple of cafes in Lake Wappapello area.

Day One
Cycle from area opposite the Lodge LEFT(north) on counter clockwise loop Hwy 143

LEFT at Des Arc on no name road with first store on your right
Continue up Gads Hill with site of Jesse James train robbery on left
LEFT on Hwy 49 to Zephyr Cafe
LEFT at Hwy B
LEFT at Hwy U
LEFT on Hwy FF
RIGHT on Hwy 34 with store on your left
LEFT at Hwy 143 back to Lodge

Day Two
Cycle from Lodge south on Hwy 143, opposite yesterday
LEFT on Hwy 34 across St. Francois River
Cross Hwy 67 "fast traffic"
Continue on Hwy 34
RIGHT at Hwy C
RIGHT at Hwy E for some hills
RIGHT for short detour into Greenville for "choice" of two cafes
Backtrack to main road
RIGHT on Hwy 67 across St. Francois River
RIGHT on Hwy FF for some very big hills
RIGHT at Patterson on Hwy 34
LEFT at hwy 143 to the Lodge

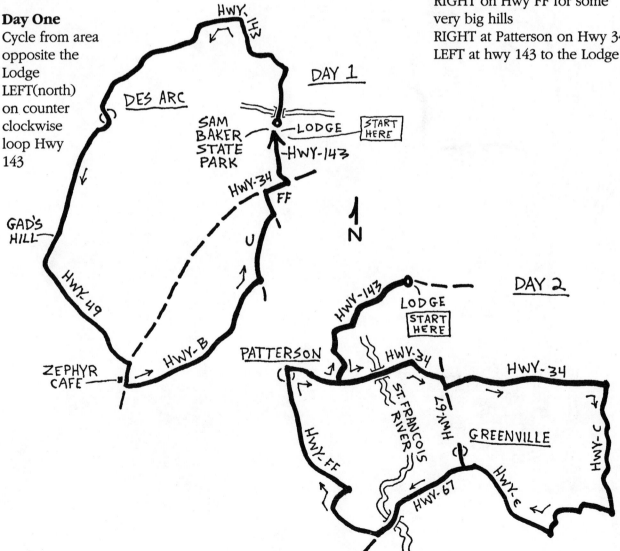

RIDE TO HERMANN

Starting Point: Union, MO City Park

Distance: 44 miles each way

Approximate Pedaling Time: 4 hours

Terrain: Hilly

Things To See: Plan this trip for two days with a layover in Hermann. The Chamber has lodging availability including many B & Bs

Cycle north from Union City Park on Hwy A
RIGHT on Hwy BB into Krakow
LEFT at Hwy YY which merges with Hwy C
RIGHT on Hwy Y through Detmold(21 miles) and Dissen(22.8 miles)
LEFT on Hwy E to Stony Hill(30.7 miles)
Cycle on Hwy E past Stony Hill
RIGHT at Hwy H to outskirts of Hermann
RIGHT at Hwy 19
LEFT on Hwy 100 into Hermann

On return trip, cycle east on Hwy 100 from Hermann
LEFT at Berger Rd
LEFT on Hwy B at Berger
LEFT on Etlah Rd
LEFT at Olive Rd
RIGHT up super hill to Wall St.
LEFT at Maupin St
Left at Hwy 100 into New Haven and Irene's Cafe (20.6 miles)
RIGHT on Hwy C
LEFT on Hwy KK
LEFT on Hwy 185 at Campbellton (28 miles)
Continue on Hwy KK
RIGHT at Four Mile Rd
RIGHT at Hwy YY through Krakow (38 miles)
RIGHT at fork on Hwy A to Unions

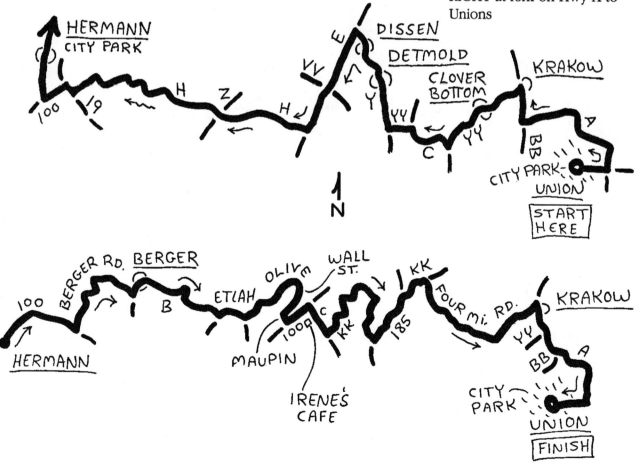

89

SILVER MINE STATE PARK LOOP

Starting Point: Silver Mines State Park near Fredricktown, Mo. I-55 South to Mo Hwy 67, exit at 72 West to Hwy D an into Park

Distance: 55 miles

Approximate Pedaling Time: 5+ hours

Terrain: Hilly

Things To See: A great ride for spring and fall says Jim Jeske. Great cafe in Ironton, food in Fredericktown, and rest stops at Silver Mines and Marble Creek Parks. This area is the Arcadia Valley of the Mark Twain National Forest.

Cycle west from point where St. Francis River crosses Hwy D
LEFT on Hwy 21 before Ironton
LEFT at Hwy E which winds east and north
LEFT at Mo Hwy 67
LEFT on Hwy 72 near Fredricktown
LEFT on Hwy D at Oak Grove

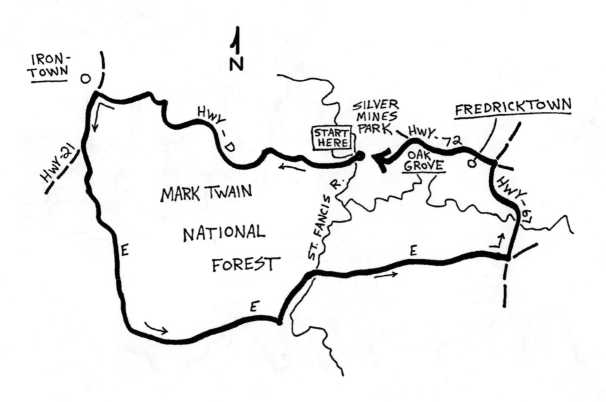

FRANKLIN COUNTY TOUR

Starting Point: Union Grade School, Union, MO
Distance: 63 miles
Approximate Pedaling Time: 5+ hours
Terrain: Hilly
Things To See: This ride is a favorite of Jim Jeske. It's all two lane, blacktop road. Food and drink are available in Krakow and New Haven.

Cycle from Union Grade School south on Rt A to Krakow
LEFT on YY through Clover Bottom
Continue straight on YY at T intersection
LEFT on Rt C at next Tee intersection and pass through Port Hudson
RIGHT at ZZ

RIGHT on Y at next Tee and continue west through Detmold and Dissen
RIGHT on Rt E
RIGHT Rt C at New Haven
Sharp LEFT on KK
RIGHT at 185 through Lyon
LEFT at YY north to Krakow
RIGHT on Rt A to Union, Missouri

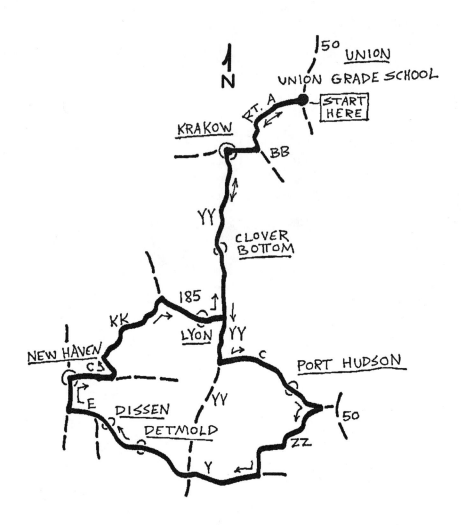

MOUNTAIN BIKING

BY SCOTT COTTER

Here in the Midwest, the closest we'll probably ever get to communing with Zen and his band of surfing buddies is to ride mountain bikes. Mountain biking, like surfing, has become somewhat of a counter culture. The clothes, music, lingo, and lifestyle all resemble that of surfing.

Despite the outward appearance of being solely for the "lunatic fringe", off-road is growing rapidly because it is attracting regular people who probably never even say, "gnarly, dude!" And, what they've learned is that mountain biking is a tremendous sport. While riding off-road, your fun meter will be pegged. Guaranteed.

Many road riders, aka roadies, have resisted mountain biking for a variety of reasons. Some don't like change. Some feel it's a sport for non-cyclists. I've even heard a roadie I ride with say it's not a real sport; only wimps do it.

The truth is, however, it's a tremendously rugged sport. Most cyclists know what the term "anarobic" means. In mountain biking, you'll become intimate friends. A guy I ride with likes to set his heart monitor close to his max heart rate so it beeps when the old ticker is really banging away. Each time we ride together I feel like I'm at a pager convention.

(IMBA RULES OF TRAIL CARTOONS) ©1992 Curt Evans & IMBA

Besides really giving the old heart a flogging, your upper body will receive it's share of hard work too. It also requires quick reflexes, coordination, and handling techniques that require strength and concentration. The benefit is a better overall condition and road handling skills.

Recently, a 15 year road veteran I know purchased a mountain bike. It has brought back his joy in cycling that he had lost. He admits to being refreshed when he gets back on his road bike. This is true for everyone because mountain and road bikes go hand in hand. Riding both will help you maintain a positive mental attitude all season long. To extend your season try off-road cycling at night. With good lights, it's a kick that is near indescribable. Watch out for deer!

The enthusiasm mountain bikers have for this sport is hard to understand if you've never experienced it before. It comes from the feeling you get when bike, rider, and mother nature come into focus and work with each other to ride some incredibly hellish terrain. Nothing compares to the high you'll get after reaching the top of a really technical, steep climb. It's a mystical feeling where you're so focused that you could do almost anything.

Before you get a bike and hit the trail, it's important to know a few things. Mountain bikes are sized and fit differently than road bikes. So spend some time with a qualified person who can help you find the right bike.

It's also important to decide what kind of off-road you'll do and how aggressive your riding will be when you match the equipment to it. Suspension is a nice feature because it reduces fatigue and soreness and will also enable you to ride tougher obstacles. The drawbacks are extra weight and increased maintenance.

And finally, when starting out, ride with experienced riders so you can learn what to do and what not to do. Don't try to follow them everywhere and do everything they do. You'll know when you've reached your limit and when it's time to back off. Now's not the time to be macho.

I've been vicitmized by macho overload before and it doesn't feel very good. Also, never ride alone. If you crash, you'll need someone to carry your carcass out of the woods.

This book is filled with great rides. Missouri boasts some great off-road places too. I urge you to seek them out and try your hand at....surfing - Midwestern style.

Mountain biking on public trails is a privilege. Follow the International Mountain Bicycling Association (IMBA) **Rules of the Trail** and everyone will enjoy the trails for many years. One irresponsible act can ruin mountain biking for all.

NATIONAL OFF-ROAD BICYCLE ASSOCIATION (NORBA)

This organization serves as another national governing organization for mountain biking. NORBA focuses primarily on off-road racing. To receive additional information or apply for membership (annual fee $25.00) write: NORBA, One Olympic Plaza, Colorado Springs, CO 80909 (719)578-4717

INTERNATIONAL MOUNTAIN BICYCLING ASSOCIATION (IMBA)
This organization promotes mountain bicycling opportunities through environmentally and socially responsible use of the land. To receive more information or apply for membership contact:
IMBA, P.O.
Box 412043, Los Angeles, CA 90041
(818)792-8830

Leave No trace!

Ride on open trails only!

Control Your Bicycle!

Always Yield trail!

PLAN AHEAD!

Never Spook Animals!

AREA MOUNTAIN BIKING TRAILS

The St. Louis area is blessed with at least six public areas suitable for mountain biking that are only a short distance from the metropolitan area. We are extremely grateful to Barb Troy, The Rivercity Pedallers and the editor of Cycling On The Move for this valuable information on where to mountain bike in the St. Louis area.

BARB TROY

despite her diminutive size is a powerhouse both on and off a bicycle. She is, without a doubt, a woman with a mission. That mission is to one day have cycling accepted as an alternative means of transportation. She first became interested in cycling in 1987 and today Barb prefers "down and dirty off road biking". She founded with the Rivercity Pedallers and the River City Tandem Connection. Barb Troy publishes the only statewide cycling newspaper, Cycling On The Move, whose mission is to inform, educate, and support cyclists.

CLAUS CLAUSSEN

discovered the sport of cycling in France in 1977. Several years later, while in the Philippines, Claus became involved in bicycle racing, a passion he still enjoys today. Claus Claussen was pleasantly surprised to find the European tradition of racing alive and well when he moved to St. Louis in 1985. Claus devotes much time and energy to bicycle racing as an active member of The St. Louis Cycling Club.

CHUBB TRAIL

CHUBB TRAIL was developed by the St. Louis County Department of Parks and Recreation and the Missouri Department of Natural Reserouces with the cooperation of the Meramec River Recreation Association. The trail is 7 miles long (14 miles round trip) but can be extended by cycling a trail along the Meramec River. The terrain is quite diverse and the Chubb Trail is not recommended for beginners.

The ChubbTrail can be accessed from I-44 west by entering either Lone Elk County Park or West Tyson County Park.

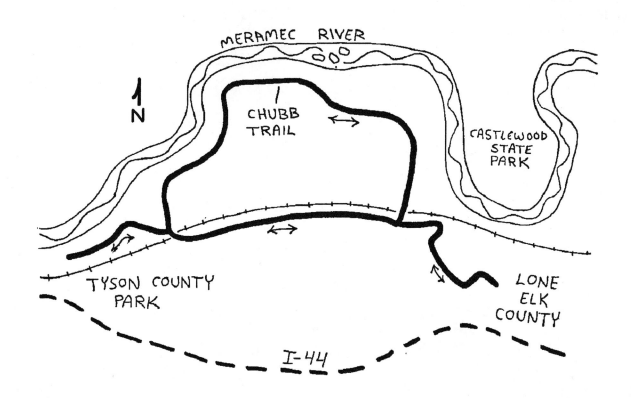

CASTLEWOOD STATE PARK

CASTLEWOOD STATE PARK is an area which straddles both sides of the Meramec River and has been a popular resort and recreation area since the early 1900s. Donations from the St. Louis Open Space Foundation have made the purchase of 1,778 acres possible for the Missouri Department of Natural Resources.

The 3-mile loop of the Grotpeter Trail is ideal for mountain biking. Additional riding can be done along the River Scene Trail with a second loop on the bluff top which presents a great vista.

Castlewood State Park may be reached from Manchester into the Park and left on Keifer Creek Road to shelter #1.

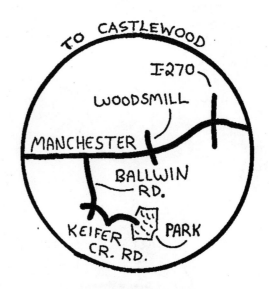

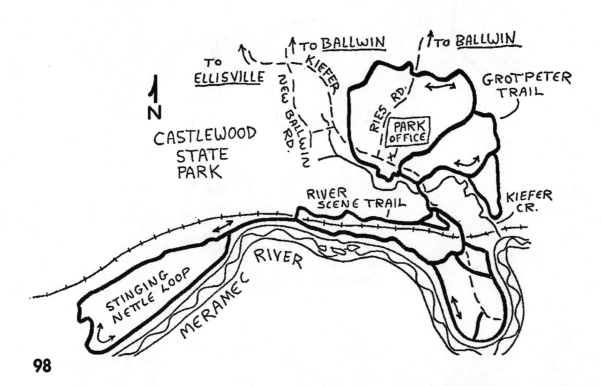

BERRYMAN TRAIL

BERRYMAN TRAIL - located in the Mark Twain National Forest, is a 24-mile national recreation trail. The Trail starts at Berryman Campground, the site of a CCC camp until the onset of World War II. The Trail is a loop course and provides the cyclist with all the challenges of mountain biking in a breath-taking forest setting. It is recommended only for self-sufficient cyclists.

To reach the Mark Twain Forest and the Berryman Trail, travel southwest on I-44 and exit to the south on Hwy 19 at Cuba. At Steelville, turn left on Rt. 8 to the Berryman trail head.

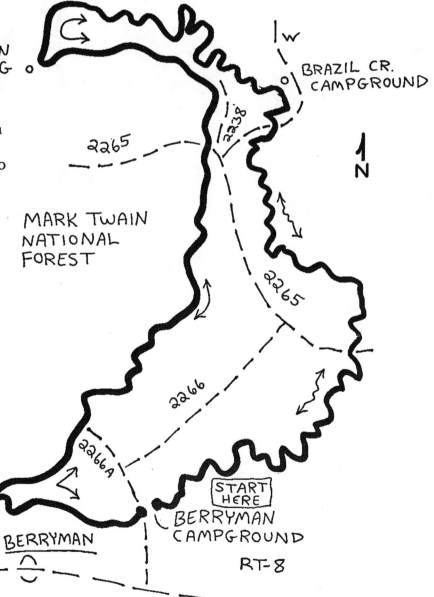

QUEENY PARK

Queeny Park is a rare urban location for "legalized" mountain biking. Although it is primarily an equestrian park, cyclists may use the same trails always giving right of way to horses.

Queeny Park is located between Weidman Rd on the west and Mason Rd on the east. It is easily reach by either I-40 or Clayton Rd, then heading south a short distance west of I-270.

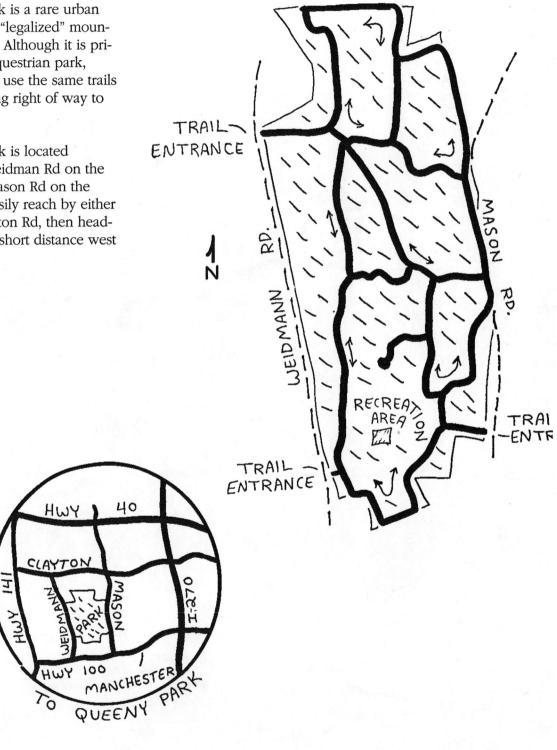

SWEET WILLIAMS NATURE TRAILS

Sweet Williams NATURE TRAILS are located at the S.I.U.E. campus. This collection of trails totals 5 miles in length. They can be reached by taking I-270 east from St. Louis and exiting north on Hwy 157. Stay left on Bluff Rd to soccer field parking lot where the trail begins.

Lost Valley Trail (map not available) is an 8-mile trail in the final completion stage. It is located in the August A. Busch Wildlife Area. This area can be reached from St. Louis by 1-70 west and then exit south at St. Charles on Hwy 94 to Weldon Springs.

ST. JOE STATE PARK

Missouri's second-largest state park - has the largest off-road area in the Midwest, with about 1600 acres for riding.

St. Joe State Park in St. Francois County can be reached by travelling south on I-55. Exit south on Hwy 67 at Festus. At the Flat River Exit take Hwy 32 west and exit left on Pimville Rd into the Park.

St. Joe State Park offers the Hickory Ridge 3-mile loop trail. Also, there's 11-mile paved portion of the Harris Branch Trail for cycling.

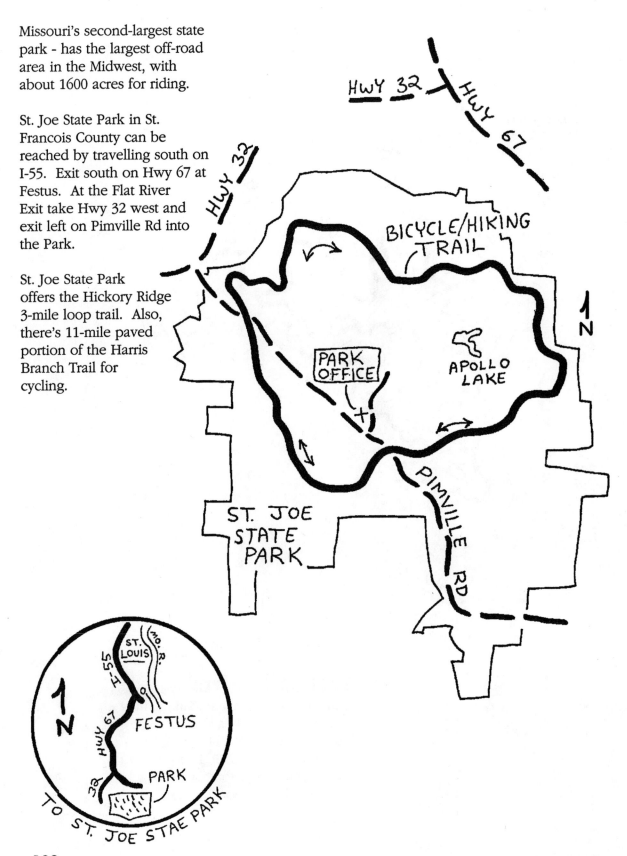

OZARK TRAIL

THE OZARK TRAIL will one day be considered the finest of its kind anywhere. It will probably be considered in the company of such greats as the Appalachian Trail. Plans were commenced in 1977 for a hiking trail to stretch from St. Louis over 700 miles into Arkansas. For information including detailed maps, contact the Missouri Department of Natural Resources, Ozark Trail Coordinator, P.O. Box 176, Jefferson City, MO 65102 (314) 751-2479

Described below are the six sections now in operation that permit mountain bikes.

As was said with the KATY Trail, use these "legal" trails for mountain biking, but don't abuse them. These are costly projects. And it's taken the energy of a hand full of cyclists to gain approval. Don't ruin it with negligence. Our legislators, many of whom have never ridden a bicycle, much less a mountain bike, won't be patient enough to consider "three times and your out". USE BUT DON'T ABUSE!

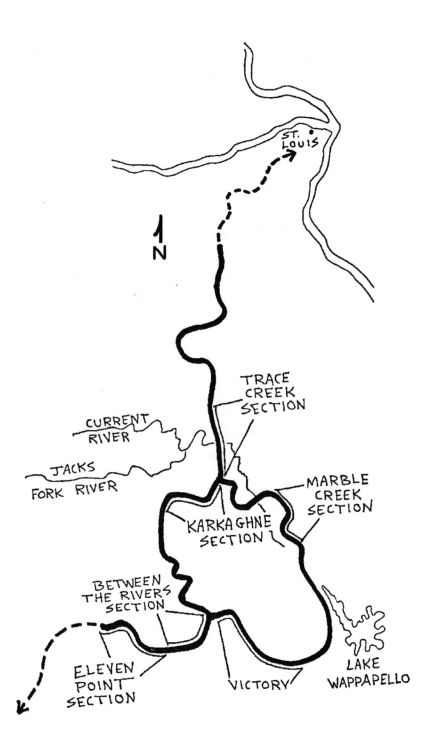

TRACE CREEK (OZARK TRAIL)

TRACE CREEK SECTION is located in Iron and Washington counties southeast of Steelville and southwest of Potosi. The northern trailhead is the Hazel Creek campground on Forest Service Rd #2408. The trail is 24 miles long crossing streams and passing through dense forests finally reaching the southern trailhead at Hwy A which marks the beginning of the Taum Sauk Section, not open to cycling.

KARKAGHNE SECTION (OZARK TRAIL)

KARKAGHNE SECTION is located in the northwest portion of Reynolds County and runs from Sutton Bluff to Hwy 72. It's about 5 miles at present and, when finished will connect Trace Creek Section with Blair Creek Section. There's an additional access point from Hwy TT

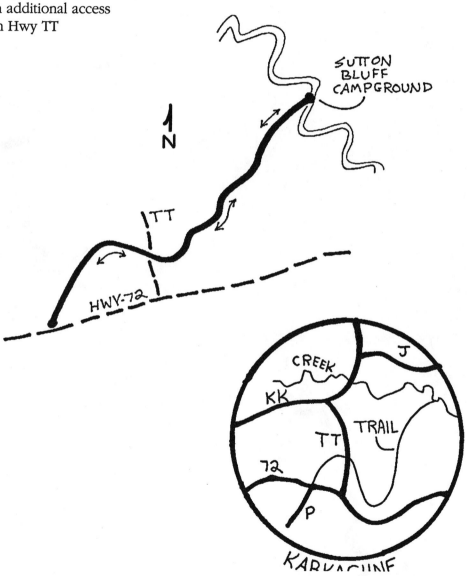

BETWEEN THE RIVERS (OZARK TRAIL)

BETWEEN THE RIVERS SEC-
TION is a 30 mile stretch located between the Current River
and the Eleven Point River.
Entry can be made near Van
Buren in Carter County at
Sinking Creek Lookout Tower
on Hwy 60, about one mile
west of Hwy J. The southern
trail head is located at the end
of the trail marked by Forest
Service Road #3152.

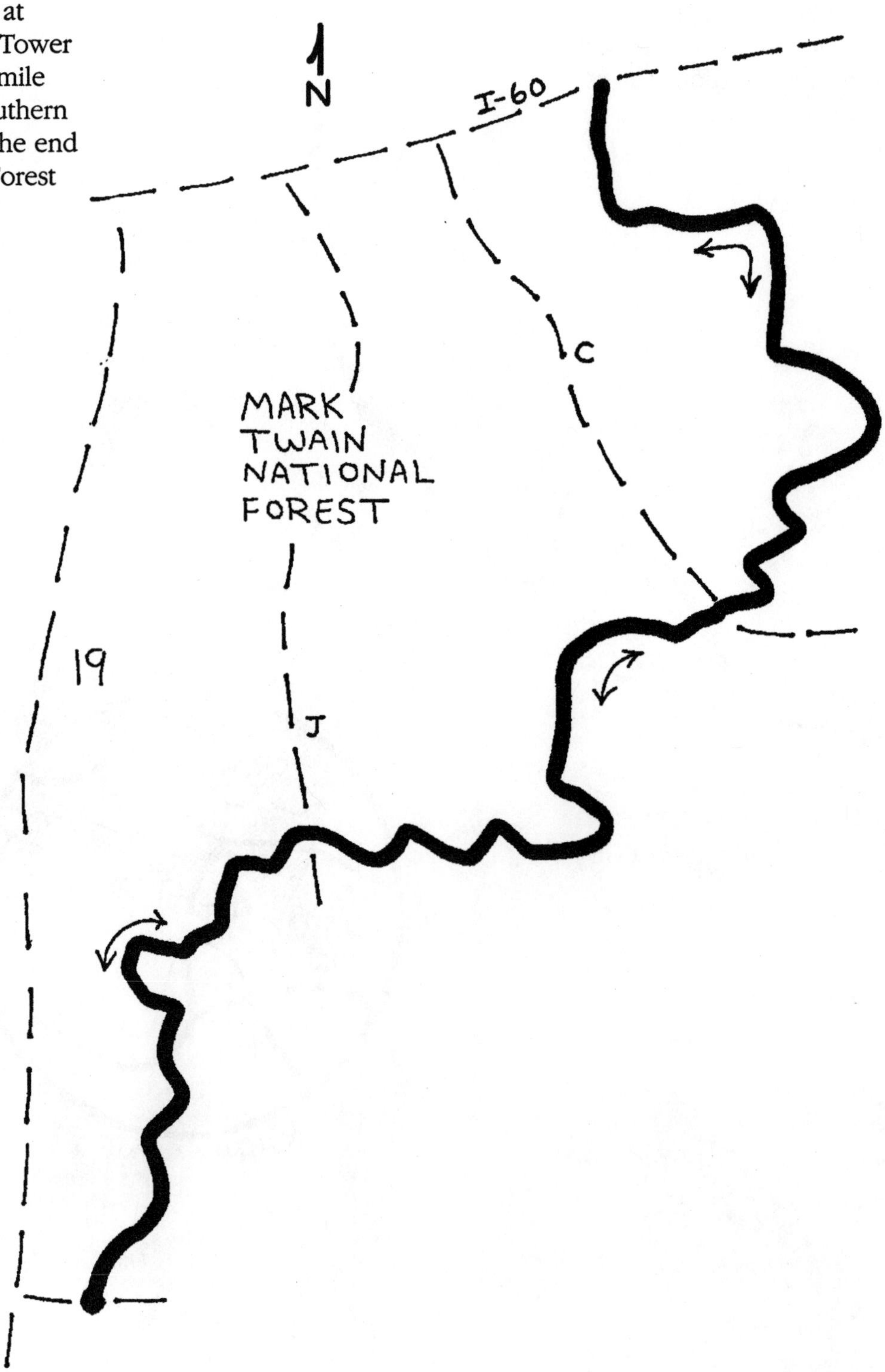

N

I-60

C

MARK
TWAIN
NATIONAL
FOREST

19

J

ELEVEN POINT RIVER SECTION (OZARK TRAIL)

ELEVEN POINT RIVER SEC-
TION is found on Forest
Service Rd 3152, in the Greer
and McCormack Lake
Recreation Areas Six miles east
of Hwy 19 and south of
Eminence. This 30-mile trail,
which lies in the heart of the
Mark Twain National Forest,
provides some rugged riding
traversing terrain of the
ELEVEN Point River and the
bluffs above.

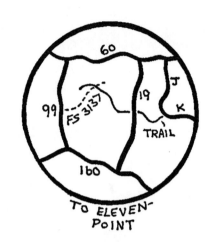

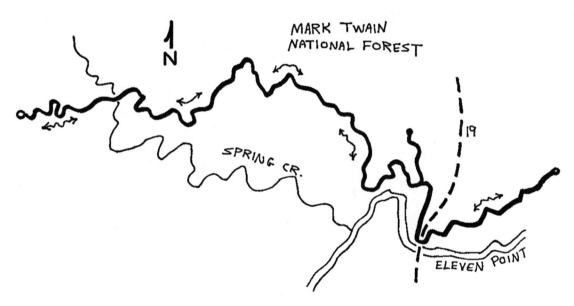

MARBLE CREEK SECTION (OZARK TRAIL)

MARBLE CREEK SECTION is located in Madison and Iron counties south of Taum Sauk and the Johnson Shut-Ins. The access to Marble Creek Campground is on Hwy E 20 miles west from Hwy 67 at Fredricktown. An 8 mile stretch of the proposed 21 mile Marble Creek Trail is open to cycling. This scenic area of Marble Creek is located in the St. Francis Mountains and gets its name from "marble" and other dolomites and sandstone bearing the name "Taum Sauk Marble".

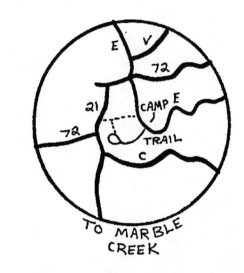

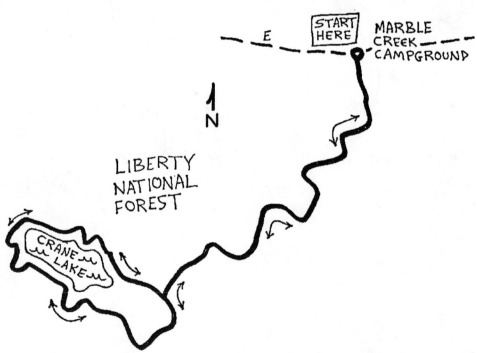

THE VICTORY SECTION (OZARK TRAIL)

VICTORY SECTION is located in Butler, Carter, and Wayne counties adjacent to Lake Wappapello State Park. Access to the trailhead is Hwy 172. Presently, 24 miles of a planned 30 mile trail is open to mountain bike traffic. Victory Trail ends in Ellsinore, Mo.

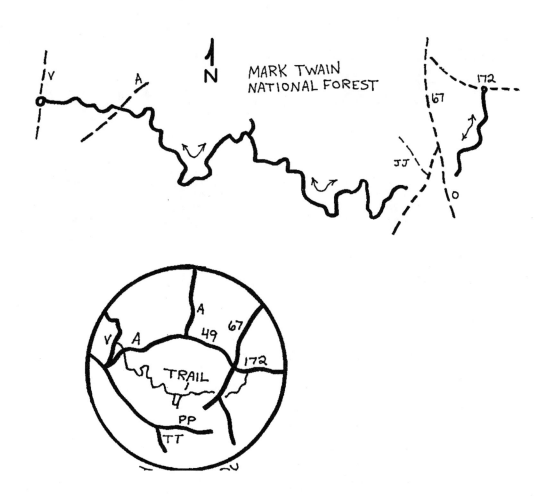

ST. LOUIS BICYCLE TRAILS

The St. Louis area is blessed with bicycle trails. These trails and projected trails are the result of public/private partnerships in most cases. These include The KATY Trail, Sam Vadalabene Great River Road Bike Trail, West Alton Trail (proposed), Riverfront Trail, Glen Carbon Heritage Trail, Lake St. Louis Hike and Bike Trail, Forest Park, and Carondelet Greenway(proposed).

It's important to note that bike paths don't enjoy the support of all the cycling community. Because they encourage two way traffic and are generally congested with traffic other than bicycles, a high incidence of bicycle accidents occur on bike paths.

Another consideration is the Missouri "side path" law. This states that if a path exists parallel to a roadway, the cyclists must use the path.

Efforts are currently being made to repeal this law. Legislators, most of whom are not cyclists, are of the misguided opinion that the roads are for motor vehicles. They legislate in favor of bicycle trails with the intention of forcing cyclists into using the trails. On the other hand, cyclists favor a **share the road** attitude.

WHY DO THEY CALL IT A BIKE PATH?

RIVERFRONT TRAIL

The Riverfront Bike Trail will ultimately extend from the Arch north to I-270. Currently about 8.75 miles are in operation.

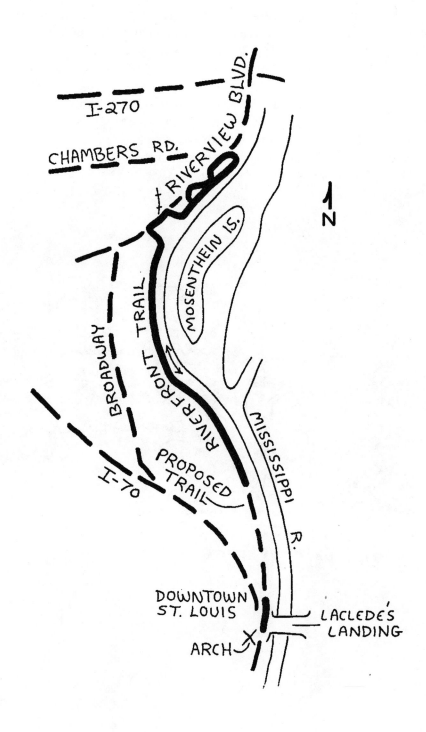

FOREST PARK

A cycle through Forest Park is rewarded with stops at The Zoo, Art Museum, Science Center, History Museum, The MUNY, and World Fair Pavilion. There are many areas just outside the Park for food, beverage, and relaxation.

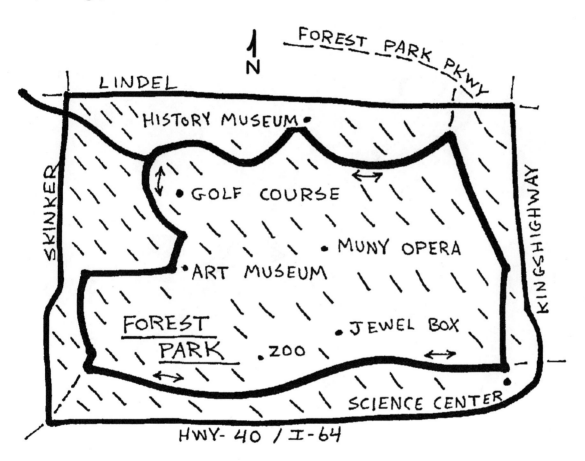

SAM VADALABENE GREAT RIVER ROAD

This popular 14 mile bike trail stretches from Alton to Grafton on the Illinois side of the Mississippi River. Longer rides can be made by using the Brussels Ferry to the Missouri side or by continuing north on the Illinois side.

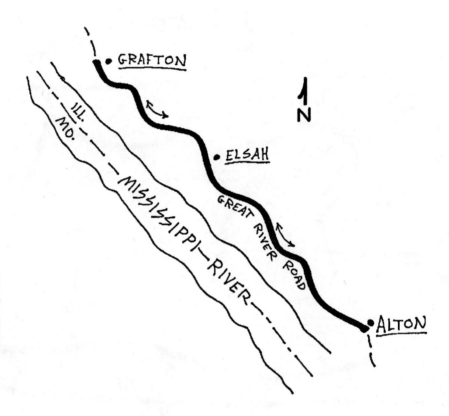

THE WEST ALTON TRAIL

The West Alton Trail project is the combined effort of Gateway Trailnet and Army Corps of Engineers to convert the Burlington Northern rail line to a bike trail. The length is 2.75
miles
stretching from the Alton side of the Mississippi to West Alton, Missouri. Donations to Gateway Trailnet (314)644-0315 can expedite this project.

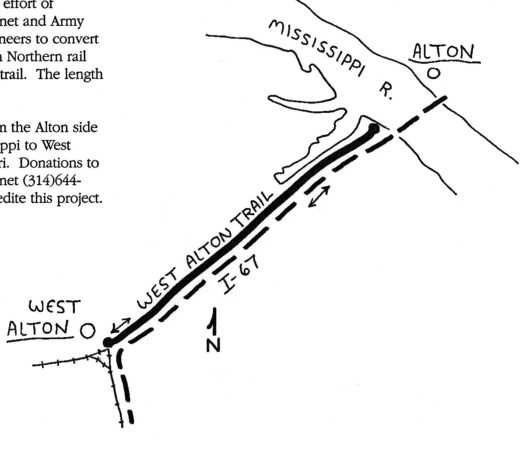

CARONDELET GREENWAY

This is another proposed railroad reclamation project by Gateway Trailnet. The trail will start at White Cliff Park, passes Grant's Farm, Clydesdale Park, and ends at I-55 and Bayless. Donations to Gateway Trailnet (314)644-0315 will also help this project.

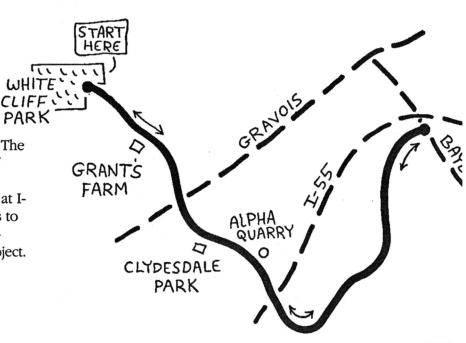

GLEN CARBON HERITAGE TRAIL

The Glen Carbon Heritage
Trail is a 3.2 mile rail-to-trail
conversion in Madison County,
Illinois. To reach this trail,
take I-270 east to Hwy 157
south .8 mile to left on Glen
Carbon Road/Main St. Turn
right immediately immediately
after Fire Dept.

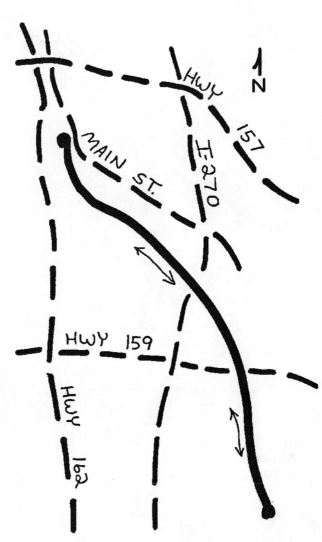

LAKE ST. LOUIS HIKE AND BIKE TRAIL

The Lake St. Louis development can be reached by I-70 west to the Lake St. Louis exit. There is a large perimeter loop and a smaller loop. Just follow the signs

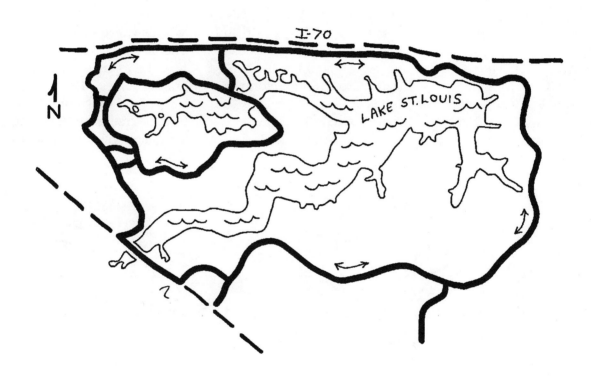

THE KATY TRAIL

THE KATY TRAIL STATE PARK began as a dream of the late investment banker, Edward D. Jones. In September 1986 Governor John Ashcroft directed the Department of Natural Resources to begin development of 200 miles of abandoned KATY rail lines to eventually stretch from Machens northeast of St. Charles westward through Jefferson City to Sedalia.

At the start of 1994, there are two major sections of the KATY Trail developed and under repair from flood damage. The eastern section starts McBaine, Rocheport, Franklin, and Booneville, a distance of more than 80 miles.

Since the KATY Trail parallels the Missouri River, much of the area was devastated by the flood of 1993. Efforts to re-open the trail are proceeding at a rapid pace. It is suggested that you call the Missouri Department of Natural Resources (800) 334-6946 and ask David Kelly for an update on the conditions of the KATY Trail. Also, current information is available by calling The Touring Cyclist location in Augusta (314) 228-4882.

ride was on a tandem.

Is there bike rental and service available?
There are both rental and service places at the trail heads. Assume there's no service en route and take spare tubes and other necessities. As traffic increases on the KATY Trail, so will the services along the trail.

What's there to see?
The KATY Trail certainly ranks near the top of Missouri's natural resources. Trains don't run up and down hills, therefore the trail is perfectly flat. This might be good news to

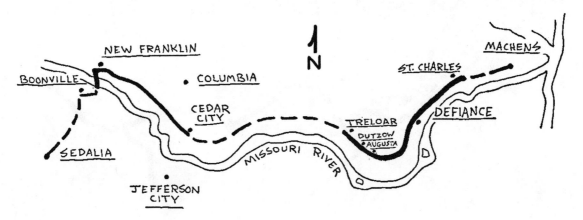

at St. Charles and continues westward paralleling Missouri Highway 94 through Weldon Spring Wildlife Area, Defiance, Matson, Augusta, Dutzow, Marthasville, and ending in Treloar, about 44 miles long.

The western section of the KATY Trail extends from Jefferson City to Sedalia passing through Hartzburg,

For the benefit of those who haven't yet cycled the KATY Trail, here area some answers to most-asked questions:

Do I need a mountain or off-road bike?
No, the trail isn't paved but the surface is firm. The larger tires of the off-road bike make the ride somewhat easier. My most pleasurable KATY Trail

newer cyclists, but makes for unchallenging riding for the rest of us. Many return from their first ride on the KATY Trail quite disappointed. It has to do with expectations. When riding the KATY Trail, take a camera, a picnic lunch, and "stop to smell the flowers". Also, leave the trail at certain points and explore the country side.

Any places to stop for food and drink?

Almost every town has a cafe, a tavern, or a general store. Several even have bed and breakfasts. At Marthasville, there's Loretta's Cafe on Two Street and Grandma's House Bed and Breakfast is on Hwy D just east of town. The Charretter Creek Winery at 304 Depot St is open for sausage, cheese, and Missouri wine.

On the western end, Hartzberg and Rocheport are quaint stops. Rocheport features one of the finest Bed & Breakfasts anywhere called The School House.

There is a winery in Rocheport and several good restaurants, one of which is The Pike Street Cafe.

The KATY Trail is one of Missouri's finest natural resources. We encourage you to **use** it but don't **abuse** it.

NEW FRANKLIN
ROCHEPORT
BOONVILLE
CEDAR CITY
STEEDMAN
CLIFTON CITY
SEDALIA
MISSOURI RIVER
JEFFERSON CITY

WEST SECTION

N

MACHENS
ST. CHARLES
WELDON SPRING
GORE
DEFIANCE
TRELOAR
MARTHASVILLE
DUTZOW
AUGUSTA
MISSOURI RIVER

EAST SECTION

119

HOW TO BUY A BIKE

Writing an article on How To Buy A Bike is an interesting challenge because when the question is posed to five veteran cyclists, you're bound to get five different answers. It's about as controversial subject as advising a friend about whether to purchase a Macintosh or a PC computer.

> My first commandment of buying a bicycle:
> **THOU SHALT NOT BUY A BICYCLE AT A STORE THAT SELLS MICROWAVES.**

In other words, seek out the expert advice of someone in a specialty bicycle store who will ask you the right questions, listen to your answers, and then will be patient and knowledgeable enough to fit you with an appropriate size and model.

Remember, if you're an adult, most bicycles can and will last a decade. Therefore, it's important that the bicycle both fit you both physically and according to your needs. The store where you buy your bicycle is most likely the place where you'll return to have it serviced. Your bicycle dealer depends upon your satisfaction, not only to return for service and accessories, but also to recommend him to others.

This article is not intended to sound as though we're preaching. We suggest you read the following pages listing area bicycle dealers, and select someone convenient for you. Then, follow the steps below keeping in mind that the service will never be as good during the shop's busy hours. A trip to get your bike repaired is not quite like passing through the drive-up window at McDonalds.

Here are three mandatory steps to follow in shopping for a bicycle:

1. *Determine the kind of riding you'll be doing and discuss it honestly with the bike dealer. If you're new, your improvement in skills will increase dramatically. Typically, less experienced customers refer to Consumer Report or some bicycle magazine for their information.*
2. *Test ride several models and always wear a helmet. Remember, you're riding a strange vehicle.*
3. *Price and style are two important components of your final decision. With the $100.00 bicycle from the discount store, you'll wind up doing most of the work. As you step up in price, the higher priced bicycle is made of lighter and more efficient components which tend to make riding easier. Consider that an additional $100.00 spent on a bicycle is only $8.33 each month for one year. You owe yourself that extra quality. Bicycle styles fall into essentially three categories: sport-touring, off-road (mountain), and cross terrain (hybrid). Off-road and tandem cycling are subjects of other articles in this Guide.*

It's not unusual today for an experienced cyclist to own both a road bike and a mountain bike. Once you've finalized that difficult decision of what bike to buy, you still need the following accessories. An approved helmet is a must, followed by a water bottle and a cage for that water bottle, a pump, a basic tool kit including a spare tube, and a comfortable saddle. Don't make the same mistake I did in preparing for my first ride. I destroyed my bike tube by over inflating it on a filling station pump. Unfortunately, it would require another chapter to tell you of other mistakes cyclists make in the early stages. Let it suffice to say, always ride with a partner or in a group until you feel very confident. Nothing's more aggravating than to throw a chain or get a flat tire with no experienced help. Many bicycle shops and tour groups conduct bicycle maintenance programs. It's like an insurance policy; it seems worthless and a waste of time until you need it.

Buying a good bicycle is the most important decision you can make right now. The rest of this Guide is meaningless without owning a good bicycle.

ST. LOUIS BICYCLE DEALERS

A-1 BICYCLE SALES	10211 Manchester Rd, Kirkwood, MO	821-0216
A & M CYCLE	4282 Arsenal, St. Louis, MO	776-1144
	Lindbergh & Long Rd, St. Louis, MO.	344-1006
ALPINE SHOP	601 E Lockwood, Webster Groves, MO	962-7229
BADEN BIKE CENTER	8204 N Broadway,St. Louis, MO	385-0364
BICYCLE HAUS	3121 Collinsville Rd, Fairmount City, IL	(618)274-3121
BICYCLE WORLD	4516 W Main, Belleville, IL	(618)642-2275
BICYCLES OF KIRKWOOD	207 N Kirkwood, Kirkwood, MO	821-3460
BIG BEND BICYCLE	8748 Big Bend Blvd, St Louis, MO	961-7331
BIG SHARK	6606 Delmar, University City, MO	862-1188
BIKE CENTERS	12011 Manchester, Des Peres, MO	965-1444
	3819 Mexico Rd, Cave Springs, MO	928-1127
	12975 Olive Blvd, Creve Coeur, MO	434-9911
	1394 Clarkson Clayton Ctr, Ellisville, MO	227-7266
	8200 Delmar, U City-Clayton, MO	727-8458
BIKES UNLIMITED	4023 Jeffco Blvd, Arnold, MO	464-2453
BREESE BIKES	3809 Pontoon Rd, Granite City, IL	(618)797-0434
THE CYCLERY	11421 St. Charles Rock Rd, Bridgeton, MO	(314)739-3030
	244 S Buchanan, Edwardsville, IL	(618)692-0070
	1231 Nedringhouse, Granite City, IL	(618)876-3456
	9 Eastgate Shopping Cntr, East Alton, IL	(618)251-4080
ENDRES	3625 W. Main, Belleville, IL	(618)233-0378
GRANADA CYCLERY & FITNESS	3139 West Clay, St. Charles, MO	946-7442
MAPLEWOOD BICYCLE	7534 Manchester, St. Louis, MO	781-9566
MESA CYCLES	7811 Clayton Rd, Clayton, MO	725-6226
REVOLUTION	175 Hilltown Village Center, Chesterfield, MO	537-4800
SOUTH COUNTY CYCLERY	9985 Lin Ferry, South County	843-5586
	2292 N Truman Blvd, Crystal City	937-6201
SOUTH SIDE CYCLERY	6969 Gravois, St. Louis, MO	481-1120
SUN & SKI SPORTS	12380 Olive, St. Louis, MO	434-9044
THE TOURING CYCLIST	301 Webster & Main, Augusta	228-4882
	11816 St. Charles Rock Rd, Bridgeton, MO	739-5183
	1101 S Big Bend Blvd, Richmond Hgts, MO	781-7973
	11701 W Florrisant Ave, Florissant, MO	921-1717
	14367 Manchester Rd, Manchester, MO	394-6477
	5809 S Lindbergh Blvd, South County, MO	894-4844
	104 South Main, St. Charles, MO	949-9630
	4632 N Highway 159, Fairview Hgts, IL	(618)233-8181
VALLEY CYCLERY	3200 N Highway 67, St. Louis, MO	921-3093
WHEELS WEST	16019 Manchester Rd., St. Louis, MO	391-8530

ORGANIZED CYCLING

Organized cycling should not be considered the opposite of disorganized cycling. When you read the biographical sketches of the contributors to this book, each found his or her way into cycling through a club or an organization. If it weren't for organized cycling, I would never have been compelled to write cycling guide books. Several months into cycling, I joined up with a Saturday morning group of about 30 cyclists. A self proclaimed leader distributed maps and then led us on a 30-40 mile journey with a pleasant stop en route for breakfast. There was neither a charge for the service nor a requirement to join the organization.

Almost every new cyclist suffers through several trips around the neighborhood or the school parking lot, before venturing forth "on the road". It's similar to learning to drive a car, although some seem never to master that skill. As a word of caution, avoid those multipurpose bike and recreation trails during your first several months of cycling. They're too narrow for oncoming bikes to pass and they're too congested with traffic from walkers, runners, skaters and others. But, this caveat certainly does not include our finest natural resource, The Katy Trail. "Bike trails" and their inherent dangers are the subject of discussion in the Bicycle Trails section.

Bicycle clubs and organizations are the life blood of cycling. Whatever your interest or skill level, there's an organization or club for you. I owe my interest in cycling to several local bicycle clubs. Their modest membership fees enabled me to make new bicycling friends and to receive a newsletter filled with cycling tours and other related cycling activities.

The following is an alphabetical listing of area bicycle clubs and touring companies:

AMERICAN YOUTH HOSTELS
7187 Manchester Road St. Louis, MO 63143 (314)644-4660. AYH was formed in 1934 as a non-profit membership organization. Its Midwest affiliate, Ozark Area Council, Inc., offers a varied program of outdoor recreations activities including bicycling. In addition to many weekly rides, OMC/AYH sponsors three annual rides, Bicycle Across Missouri (BAM), Cycle Across Missouri Parks (CAMP), and the Moonlight Ramble.

BELLEVILLE AREA BICYCLING & EATING SOCIETY (BABES)
Contact Ray Latimer (618)628-0518 for information about Wednesday night rides. BABES covers the entire Metro East sector and has contributed many routes to this guide.

BREAK AWAY BICYCLE TOURS
Contact Larry Brinker (618)876-9118 P.O. Box 69188 St. Louis, MO 63169. Offers a variety of tours ranging from Bike/Hike weekends to road tours to off road mountain biking. Some tours include B & Bs or rustic lodges. Custom tours may be arranged. Brochures are available upon request.

MISSOURI MEANDERS, MEANDER THE U.S., & MOME LITE
are all names synonymous in the St. Louis area with fun cycling. The rides are famous for beautiful routes, great food and friendly people. Trips range from single day rides to week long trips in the California Wine Country and the Natchez Trace. For a free brochure contact Julie Wynn (314) 849-4326

PEDAL PUSHERS BICYCLE CLUB

Founded by the late Joe Spencer. Organized rides Tuesday and Thursday at 6:00 P.M. and Saturday at 9:00 A.M. from Pedal Pushers Bike Shop, 616 Franklin Ave. Edwardsville, IL 62025 Contact Mike Chapman or Jean Spencer (618)656-7701

THE RIVERCITY PEDALLERS

11358 Manchester; Kirkwood, MO 63122 (314)965-8999. Rides tailored to the needs of all kinds of cyclists including on road and off road. A very personal, hands-on approach. Membership includes Cycling On The Move newspaper mailed home plus discounts at Bike Center stores.

ST. LOUIS BICYCLE TOURING SOCIETY(SLBTS)

11816 St. Charles Rock Rd, Bridgeton, MO 63044 (314)739-5180. The Touring Society is sponsored by The St. Louis Bicycle Touring Cyclist. At the start of each season, the Touring Society publishes a calendar of local, national, and international tours it organizes. It plays an important role in advocacy to promote better cycling for everyone. Tailwinds, the newsletter of the Touring Society is published ten times each year and, the Touring Society maintains an 24-hour information line (314) 851-0900.

The following is a partial list of names and addresses of national organizations which serve the specialized needs of bicyclists.

Bicycle Federation of America
1818 R St., NW, Washington, DC 20009
Promotes all aspects of cycling, publishes Pro Bike News, conducts research on safety and bike-trail planning.

Bikecentennial
P.O.Box 8398, Missoula, MT 59807
National non-profit group promotes touring, leads extended bike tours. An annual membership fee of $22.00 entitles one to 9 issues of BikeReport magazine, more than 19,000 miles of bicycle routes through Cyclosource catalog, the Cyclists' Yellow Pages reference book, and a wide selection of on- and off-road tours.

International Randonneurs
727 N. Salina St., Syracuse, NY 13224
Organization for long-distance cycling; sponsors U.S. qualifying rides for Paris-Brest-Paris event.

League of American Wheelmen(LAW)
Suite 209, 6707 Whitestone Rd., Baltimore, MD 21207. The oldest U.S. cycling organization and a major advocacy group. Membership open to everyone.

National Off-Road Bicycle Association (NORBA) serves as the national governing organization for mountain biking. An annual membership fee of $25.00 affords members eligibility for all NORBA races, an off-road competition guide, 12 monthly issues of NORBA News, insurance at NORBA races, and an opportunity to participate in mountain bike clinics. NORBA, One Olympic Plaza, Colorado Springs, CO 80909   (719)578-4717

Rails to Trails Conservancy
1400 16th St., NW, Washington, DC 20036
National organization that promotes conversion of disuse railroad beds to hiking/biking trails. The KATY Trail is a part of this program.

The Tandem Club of America
c/o Jack Goetz, 2220 Vaness Dr., Birmingham, AL 35242 Sponsors events, publishes a newsletter

U.S. Cycling Federation
1750 E. Boulder St., Colorado Springs, CO 80909. Oversees amateur bicycle racing and Olympic training.

An explanation of bicycle advocacy simply means making your community more "bicycle-friendly". Both novice and veteran cyclists quickly appreciate the challenges of sharing the road with other vehicles.

Bicycle advocacy is nothing new. The League of American Wheelmen (LAW), the nation's oldest bicycle advocacy group, was founded in the 1880s. As a member of LAW, The St. Louis Cycling Club was formed In 1888 making it the oldest cycling club in American. The L.A.W. established its Good Roads Campaign to improve roads for all users. In 1890, the League boasted nearly 100,000 members.

The L.A.W. Good Roads Campaign was so successful that it helped to increase the popularity of the automobile which subsequently brought about the decline in the bicycle as a means of transportation.

Today, we're witnessing what many call the second golden age" in cycling. Unfortunately, neither road construction nor transportation legislation have kept pace with the increase in bicycle usage. The Federal Transportation Act of 1991 is the first serious legislation enacted to address the problems of bicyclists and pedestrians.

The Intermodal Surface Transportation Efficiency Act (ISTEA) has mandated that each state name a bicycle-pedestrian coordinator.

Missouri is fortunate to have Dennis Scott as bicycle-pedestrian coordinator. Dennis operates within the jurisdiction of the Missouri Highway and Transportation Department. Dennis Scott is a cyclist who has logged more than 250,000 miles. He is accessible and knowledgeable and can be reached by writing Dennis Scott, Missouri Bicycle-Pedestrian Coordinator, Missouri Highway and Transportation Dept. Planning Division, P.O. Box, Jefferson City, MO 65102

Local and state advocacy contacts include:

Gateway Trailnet
7185 Manchester Rd, St. Louis, MO 63143
Contact: Ted Curtis (314)644-0315
Gateway Trailnet, a regional land trust formed in 1988 by private citizens with the assistance of the City of St. Louis and McDonnell Douglas employees, is a nonprofit organization directly involved in land conservation. Trailnet's mission is to identify and help develop greenways (linear parks), trails, and bicycle paths throughout the St. Louis metropolitan area. A high priority for Trailnet is the conversion of abandoned railroad rights-of-way into scenic trails. Three major projects include the Riverfront Trail, the West Alton Trail, and the Carondelet Trail. Gateway Trailnet invites volunteers of time, talent, and dollars.

Missouri Bicycle Federation
P.O. Box 104871, Jefferson City, MO 65110
A nonprofit cycling advocacy group founded in March of 1993. The group has statewide representation that speaks as a united body for or against issues affecting cyclists. MBF's mission is to make Missouri a better place to ride through the advancement of bicycle access, safety, and education. Any cyclist who shares similar thoughts should contact the Missouri Bicycle Federation at (314)636-4488. The newsletter, The HUB, is very informative on these matters.

These advocacy organizations depend upon your input and your support to make the St. Louis area more "bicycle-friendly". There are more opportunities for cyclists to improve their position in the transportation world today than ever before.

If you are interested in other bicycle and pedestrian issues at a national level, contact one of the following:

Don't complain about the plight of cyclists. There are so many advocacy groups available today at the local, state, and national level. Stand up and be counted. Make your voice heard.

The League of American Wheelmen(LAW)
190 W. Ostend St., Suite 120
Baltimore, MD 21230
(410) 539-3399
Specializes in rallies, bicycle club activities and advocacy at the national and local level.

Bikecentennial
P.O. Box 8308
Missoula, MT 59807
(406) 721-1776
Specializes in bicycle touring, mapping, long distance bicycle routes and advocacy.

Rails-to-Trails Conservancy
1400 16th St. NW, Suite 300
Washington, DC 20036
(202) 797-5400
Promotes the conversion of abandoned railroad corridors to multi-use trails.

Bicycle Federation of America
1818 E St. NW, Washington, DC 20009
Promotes walking and bicycling as efficient and environmentally friendly transportation modes. The National Bicycle and Pedestrian Advocacy Campaign is a BFA project supported by grants from several foundations.

BIBLIOGRAPHY

The following is a partial list of books available on cycling. They are in random order and available only at full line book stores, some bicycle stores, and major libraries. On several of the major titles, we have included addresses. A (✔) mark indicates books we've particularly enjoyed.

The Cyclists' Yellow Pages, Bikecentennial, P.O. Box 8308, Missoula, MT 59807. A complete directory to everything related to cycling. (✔)

The Bicyclist's Source Book by Leccese and Plevin, $16.95, Woodbine House, 5615 Fishers Lane, Rockville, MD 20852. As complete a bicycle reference book as we've found.(✔)

Effective Cycling by John Forester, $17.95, MIT Press, 55 Hayward St., Cambridge, MA 02142. Considered by most to be the bible of cycling. Available also in videotape. (✔)

The Bicycle Repair Book by Rob Van der Plas

The Bicycle Touring Manual by Rob Van der Plas, $16.95

Training For Cycling by Davis Phinnery and Connie Carpenter

Anybody's Bike Book by Tom Cuthbertson, $9.95, An original manual of bicycle repairs.

Bike Touring, The Sierra Club Guide to Outings on Wheels, $10.95

Bicycle Magazine's Complete Guide, $16.95 (✔)

Bicycle Magazine Cycling Series, Rodale Press, 33 E. Minor St., Emmaus, PA 18098
- Cycling For Women
- Bicycle Repair
- Bicycle Touring
- Easy Bicycle Maintenance
- Fitness Through Cycling
- Mountain Bikes
- Ride Like A Pro
- Riding and Racing Techniques
- Training For Endurance

Glenn's New Complete Bicycle Manual by Clarence Coles and Harold Green, $23.00

Richards' Ultimate Bicycle Book by Richard Ballantine and Richard Grant, $29.95 (✔)

Fat Tire Rider, Everyone's Guide to Mountain Biking by Kennedy, Kloser, & Samer $19.95

Complete Book of Bicycling by Greg LeMond, $11.00

Cycling - A Celebration of the Sport and the World's Best Places to Enjoy It by Arlene Plevin, $12.00

The Complete Book of Bicycling by Eugene A Sloan, $15.95

CAST OF CHARACTERS

STEVE KATZ-
AUTHOR

PHIL SHOULBERG-
PHOTOGRAPHER

RANDY SEBA-
GRAPHIC
DESIGN &
LAYOUT

MIKE OGDEN - MAPMAKER

BOB BLISS - CARTOONIST